Girl's Guide to the English Public Schoolboy

Rebecca Irvine retired from a short but vivid career as a Public Schoolboy's moll in the mid-80s. She is now rumoured to be a sedate researcher and writer living somewhere between W11 and West Galway.

Goose,
being home seems to be a state of mind (if you cant beat 'em join em) & Keep a record so you can escape & giggle in retrospect!

REBECCA IRVINE

A Girl's Guide to the English Public Schoolboy

Mandarin

A Mandarin Paperback

A GIRL'S GUIDE TO
THE ENGLISH PUBLIC SCHOOLBOY

First published in Great Britain 1983
by Enigma Books, an imprint of Severn House Publishers Ltd
First paperback edition published 1985
by Severn House Publishers Ltd
This edition published 1990
by Mandarin Paperbacks
Michelin House, 81 Fulham Road, London SW3 6RB

Mandarin is an imprint of the Octopus Publishing Group

A CIP catalogue record for this title
is available from the British Library
ISBN 0 7493 0493 6

Printed in Great Britain
by Cox & Wyman Ltd, Reading

Illustrations by Nicola Jennings

To my dear brother Jim,
who is much maligned in these pages
– with my love

Contents

Introduction

Someone once said there are those who are born to greatness, those who achieve it and those who have it thrust upon them, or words to that effect. Public Schoolboys happen to one in much the same way. Being born to them means they run in the family, achieving them has a lot to do with having sons, and having them thrust upon you means that, for some reason you may never recall, you wake up next to one in the morning.

Like greatness, learning to live with a Public Schoolboy is not easy, especially if you are new to the breed. They are a strange race used to inhabiting rarified atmospheres and like all aliens they have problems coping with run-of-the-mill humanoids – that is, those who haven't been to the same school. Unfortunately, this means that even in these enlightened days, they have problems with 99.8% of the female race. As if that weren't enough they labour under the convenient delusion that it is the girls who are odd.

The aim of this book is to help girls of all backgrounds prepare for the pitfalls they will doubtless encounter if they are careless enough to lose their hearts to members of this rare and increasingly threatened species. Why bother? Well, some girls *must* lose their hearts in this reckless fashion in the interests of humanity, and they need all the help they can get, poor dears. After all, the Public Schoolboy is as English as muffins, as much part of our heritage as plus-fours and bowler hats and for that reason should be preserved. This may be in direct conflict with the egalitarian ideals of our age, but I should like to point out that nowadays good old GB has precious few assets to flaunt, and the only thing she is global brand leader of is eccentrics. The world looks to us to produce them, and we must not let it down; and I defy anyone to point to a better producer of 22 carat eccentrics than the English Public School. So though the system may be sexist, elitist and even anachronistic it has its place and must be kept stocked. This is where some women come in, biology being what it is, and it is for these selfless heroines that I write.

At which point I had better admit that within these pages you will find some of the grossest generalisations in history – I admit it to save you the bother of writing to complain. Sorry chaps. It has to be that way because even after many shockingly frank and free discussions with Public Schoolboys' wives, girlfriends, sisters, mothers and lovers, I have to admit that there is no such thing as the definitive version, just an awful lot of quirks that most examples have in common. Oh, and please remember at all times that the Guide is meant to be affectionate, even though it may not always seem so at first glance.

Finally, the most important aim of this book is to spread hope and light among all girls involved with Public Schoolboys wherever they are; I know from acid experience that in the early stages you need as much of these two commodities as you can get. Indeed, sometimes the outlook can be so hopelessly dark that it doesn't seem worth going on – but don't give up too easily: once won such men can be a girl's best friend.

The fact that the English Public Schoolboy frequently regards his dog as *his* best friend should warn you that you'll never have a really meaningful relationship with him unless your bark isn't nearly so good as your bite.

Faintly Historical Note

When things are at their blackest, and a conviction that one is in love with a dangerous deviant of criminal bent grips the spine, remember this: popular mythology would have us believe that the Public School was devised pretty much as an Upper Class Borstal for those obviously destined to become skeletons in ancestral closets. I have always found this comforting, though I confess I'm not sure why. Possibly it has something to do with the cosiness of knowing that when the modern-day replicas start to fling blancmange at each other and the odd Turner water-colour they are merely upholding ancient tradition.

Actually, each individual institution has its own raison d'être, some holy and others wholly banal. Whatever the terms of the foundation, however, it must be admitted that the conditions in Public Schools seemed at one time to have been designed to keep in check those blue blooded young sports who shot the family tutor before brekker and then ate him on toast with gentleman's relish. In some places an intimate dormitory slept a mere forty, with bars at the window to lend a pleasingly penitential air, while at others the young offenders were allotted cells so tiny that they had to fold their beds into the wall to open their wardrobes. As for food, well! There were those sisters who, adjured to think of the starving millions as they pushed their potatoes aside, thought dear nanny must be referring to the Boys, so dire were the tales of malnutrition sent back by their siblings.

Happily, for one reason and another, things have changed. Boys are now usually sent to Public School for a Good All Round Education rather than to be cured of nasty habits, and academic standards are generally very high. Also, if you are now woefully picturing the boy you love ekeing out his youth in a cavernous dorm, the chances are that your concern is wasted. Conditions are no longer basic-basic and the food is pretty good too. My own brother, for instance, spent five years inhabiting a rather nifty little penthouse with a charming view of the Surrey countryside and excellent full board thrown in. My dear papa joyfully coughed up the rent as part of the fees. With conditions like these at school, the dear child is forced to look elsewhere to exercise his Complaint Gland, and frequently settles on the family home as an appropriate spot. Ah, well.

By and large, the above mentioned changes are welcomed by both boys and parents, since it is now generally acknowledged that relative comfort does not a milksop make. Conversely there are still those few who deplore latter-day laxness and view it as palpable proof that Britain is no longer great. The whole thing worries them sick, and they get frightfully worked up as the following sad tale amply illustrates.

One member of the Old Brigade became so incensed by this trend towards liberalism that he was moved to pen a letter to *The Times*. He had, he wrote, scoured the length and breadth of the land in search of a Prep School for his son but found none suitable; they all had central heating. He didn't have any such nonsense in his own home, he roared, and as a result his boy was a tough little bruiser who could stand anything. Why should he be ruined and softened up at school? What was the government going to do about it? Didn't they care that the flower of the nation's youth was being press-ganged into cissydom, that was what he wanted to know. Fortunately the letter was never published, so Her Majesty's Ministers were left untroubled by the hornet's nest this tortured lament would doubtless have stirred up.

PART ONE

Basic Grounding

In common with most people in the English speaking world I was brought up to believe that one should always begin things at the beginning. There are times when this advice has seemed frankly fatuous to me, but this is not one of them. The prospect of guiding the unsuspecting through the troubled water of a romance with a Public Schoolboy is so daunting that I quite simply can't decide where the start really is. The best solution, it seems to me, is to fall back on that time honoured refuge of the reluctant sage and throw the question over to the other side.

Is This The Real Thing?

Be honest. Are you really sure that you care deeply enough about the Public Schoolboy in your life to tackle a gruelling course of study which will be more intellectually and philosophically frustrating than O-level maths? Do you really have a burning urge to understand and unravel the labyrinthine twists of his mind? In short, is this your vocation?

Before you answer, let me assure you that whatever you decide, no judgement on your character rests upon this issue. In other words, if you know in your heart of hearts that your Public Schoolboy represents no more than a passing aberration of taste, no-one will blame you. On the contrary, those on the other side of the great dividing line will probably regard you as a shining example of the Practical Girl, and be rather jealous.

For you, lucky lady, are at liberty to lie back and enjoy it, if you'll forgive the unintentional pun. You can laugh your way through to his heart, mock his mawkishness and prick his vanity whenever it takes your fancy. Why, you can even admit to being a feminist without fear of reprisal. You can shrug off the bad breath, and turn a blind eye to the sandwiches filled with cold baked beans, instant hot chocolate powder and mayonnaise, in the exhilarating knowledge that you won't have to put up with them for too long. In short, you are free to enjoy the finer points of the liaison, whatever *they* are, without succumbing to the gnawing doubt that the man might be happier at Whipsnade (as an exhibit) rather than even trying to adapt himself to modern society.

Whereas those among us who feel dread destiny has met us with our match can allow no such self-indulgent ease. Instead we must try to understand and sympathise, which – honestly – is not easy. Quite the reverse, actually.

So I challenge you, gentle reader, to hold a mirror up to your soul. Do you see lasting love or passing lust? Only you will know the answer, but if the exercise proves beyond reasonable doubt that you are one of the doomed few, you'd better read on. You poor chump.

The Naming of Parts

Before we begin this voyage into the kingdom of lesser heroes I think it would be appropriate to give the General-All-Purpose-English-Public-Schoolboy a name, for the sake of brevity as much as anything else. So from now on he will be referred to as Jenkins.

I know this may seem a cold and unfriendly name to give to the fellow, but he will be quite happy wth it himself. It would be totally wrong to call him Tom, Dick or Harry anyhow, since most have very quaint names like Tristram and Miles in real life and try not to use them. Also, he will probably be more comfortable with his surname, since this is the way he has known himself since his schooldays. It may sound far-fetched, but I actually met a Jenkins once who, returning home after his first term at Prep School, suffered paroxysms of angst because no-one seemed to be talking to him. As the days wore on his face grew longer and his unhappiness deeper. He regarded his family with an increasingly baleful gaze, which unsettled them quite a bit. After a week of this his father brought matters to a head. Thumping his fist on the dinner table so hard that the china did a tango he said 'Look, Tristram, I understand that the first term away can be hard, but for goodness sake *tell* us about it!'

Jenkins who knew by now that the penalty of speaking out of turn was chocolate deprivation, placidly pronged a pea and said nothing. His mother shed a silent tear.

'Tris*tram*,' bellowed his father, cuffing him gently the while, '*Speak* when you're spoken to!'

'But I didn't think you were,' whispered the bewildered child.

'You are the only Tristram in the room, aren't you? I mean, you are my only son and your name *is* Tristram Jenkins, isn't it?' thundered his enraged patriarch.

Bells rang. Pennies dropped. Jenkins T, the school register ran. T stood for Tristram. So he hadn't been sent to Coventry after all. With a joyful whoop he leapt back into the bosom of his family.

This cautionary tale should help you to understand

'Your name is Tristram Jenkins, isn't it?'

why Jenkinses, as a rule, refer to their fellows by their last names when they grow up.

A Jenkins By Any Other Name

As with all rules, there are exceptions. In this case, the deviation from the norm occurs when two Jenkinses are very good friends in which case human frailty, even at public school, tends to manifest itself in an endearment. It's easy enough for the rest of us, who can refer to loved ones as darling, shorten each other's first names and so on, but it is a very different matter for Jenkins. This is largely because any sign of emotion or affection connotates cissyness. Hence a peculiarly confusing code has emerged. Bear with me.

The simplest example is when the close associate of a double-barrelled boy, a Jenkins-Smythe for example, drops the first barrel and addresses him as Smythe. If this is tolerated it means that the two are practically blood brothers, whereas anyone else using the shortened form will swiftly be made aware that he presumes far, far too much. Another token of affection is to add a syllable, as in Smyth-ie. Yet another variation on the theme is to forget all of this and invent a nickname, which for safety's sake must always be derogatory.

To add insult to injury, the problem is compounded when the boys leave school. Society is now so informal that people tend to refer to each other by their first name, viz. Tristram and Miles etc. In an exemplary piece of double-think, Jenkins perceives this as a formal title, a sign of respect, the required norm. Only a chosen few are allowed to refer to him by his surname or its derivative, and all others doing so are regarded as shameless interlopers. I did warn you it was confusing.

As a girl you will normally be expected to use the

formal (sorry, informal) title i.e. Tristram, Miles etc. If you can't take such a rigid approach you may be permitted to invent your own nickname. Should this fantastic honour be conferred on you, remember it will find no favour if it is not insulting: 'Skunk' will do, but 'Bunny-kins' is a complete no-no.

Oh, and when it comes to nicknames and such like, for heaven's sake be sensible. My friend Jessica once grew terribly fond of a Jenkins, though possibly not quite as fond as he might have wished. She explained the delicate nature of her feelings, and he, manfully cutting his losses, told her that if she only loved him in a brotherly sort of way, that was grand as he'd always wanted a little sister, and thereafter he referred to her as L'il Sis. Some time later, Jessica had occasion to telephone Jenkins at home, for he had fallen off his horse and broken an elbow. After a progress report the lady who had answered the call asked Jess if she could tell the patient who had called. 'Oh,' said the dear girl blithely, 'just tell him it's L'il Sis.'

'But he's only got an elder sister,' came the reply after an icy pause. 'Or at least I thought he had. Da-*dee!*'

It was touch and go for a couple of hours, I gather, but the family held together in the end. Yet as Jessica says, when you're dealing with a Jenkins, 'That chap who asked what's in a name as if it didn't matter must have been a total blithering idiot!'

Homework

Quite the best way to start to plumb the mysteries of a Jenkins and all his tribe is to have one for a brother. This way you can follow his progress closely and become familiar with the effect a Public School education has on a child. To be perfectly honest there is no real substitute for this invaluable training.

However, if you should be brotherless or have parents who for political or financial reasons have elected to send their male progeny to state school, don't despair: you can always borrow one. This is quite acceptable since most sisters I know will lend out siblings free of charge, mainly to get some peace and quiet. If this fails, rent one. Most of the little darlings will do anything, even talk to a girl, in exchange for a bottle of beer, a new record album or a used copy of Men Only.

The best time for field study is the shortest break between two solid blocks of education, the time that state schools refer to as half-term. Ah, and before we proceed a step further, let me reiterate that you must get your terminology right. Most Public Schools go to ludicrous lengths to avoid the term 'term' and have Halves, or Quarters, or something instead. This can be confusing I know, but if you get it wrong you will be subject to howls of derision and deemed too stupid to bother with, though your CV be monumentally impressive. Also, resist the temptation to be side-tracked by the improper fractions. It is no business of yours to wonder if it is really right to have three Halves in one year, or, come to that, what happened to the fourth Quarter. Suffice it to say that there is a method in the madness and even if there isn't you aren't here to upset the apple cart.

The reason for choosing this time is that it is only then that Jenkins at home most resembles his school self. During the longer breaks mothers begin to exert a civilising influence, gradually fumigating the boy and battering him into saying please and thank you at the appropriate times. (This latter is not usually achieved until late in the summer holidays, for throughout his adolescence Jenkins communicates in mono-phrases unless he is talking to his contemporaries, or maybe a favoured dog.)

During the short breaks, mamma tends to be lenient. She is so pleased to find the boy in one piece and with no limbs in plaster, that strange bodily aromas and general brutishness are dismissed as a phase. For during term- (or whatever) time the poor woman lives in fear and dread, so legion are the disasters a boy can encounter while away. One lady I knew, the mother of an old boyfriend of mine, told me that she used to answer the telephone with great trepidation whenever Jenkins was at school, for at least once a term he would break an arm or a leg, or failing that, amuse himself by dislocating a toe or burning off both eyebrows. It was only during longer breaks that she wished he'd break his neck, instead of the french windows for a change. This line of thinking is common to many mums.

The reason for seeing the boys in something as close to their natural state as possible, is that when they are older you can appreciate how much they have improved rather than live in despair because you have fallen in love with an ape. You see, most of the more unpalatable habits of youth persist into later life. The saving grace, as far as you are concerned, is that the odd one or two don't. In other words, prepare to thank the Lord for small mercies. Big ones, I'm afraid, are off.

Test

Learn the term for 'term' at the top ten Public Schools of the year. If you are unsure of the relative positions on the league table, phone *The Tatler* magazine and ask them, for they're terribly useful for this sort of thing. Should it be that your chap is not an alumnus of one of these, find out the jargon for his old school too.

Members of the Class

Pick a school photograph, any school photograph, as the card sharps say, and what do you see? If the school is a public one you will be looking at an artistic disaster portraying six hundred or so unhealthily neat boys, a bit of what look likes a Victorian urinal, and a smattering of masters who don't look at all well. The game is to spot little Jenkins, and believe you me it's not as easy as it sounds. I mean, *is* cloning a scientific black-hole of the future or has something been happening in the playing fields of academe that we haven't been told about? I wonder, I really do, when I consider how many hours I have spent trying to locate my own brother on one of those charmless miniatures. Surely if all was well it wouldn't be that difficult – after all, I'm the doting sister who used to change his nappy.

It must be that some sort of mystical symbiosis occurs when the boy joins the school with the result that he looks exactly like everyone else there – give or take an inch or two and the odd errant blackhead. What price Nature v. Conditioning now, eh?

A visit to the school compounds the identity problem, because they all sound alike too. Each uses the same vocabulary, and if you don't think that should be too much for the average English speaking female, you are simply too naïve for your own good. Go on, admit it, you didn't know 'wuggas' was a code word for Angel Delight, now did you? The only thing that eases the pain is the glad news that Jenkins tends to be terse, and therefore does not need a lot of words, so with application, anyone can be fully conversant in his tongue in twenty minutes or less.

All of this may lead you to assume that every Jenkins is the fruit of upper middle-class loins with a few aristocratic genes thrown in, if only because these are the types who regularly mutilate the language anyhow. Logical though the deduction be, however, it is not strictly accurate, for reasons I shall now divulge.

Potted History

Before you attempt this section be warned that it should not be tackled by anyone in a frivolous mood. It is complex, serious, relevant and therefore tedious beyond belief. I will try to skate over it as quickly as possible. Are you sitting comfortably? . . .

Right. The root cause of the whole Public School shebang was a chap called William of Wykeham. This worthy vicar took it into his head that paupers were not necessarily as light between the ears as they were in the pocket and might get along a lot better if they could speak Latin (a curious notion I grant you, but things were very different in those days), so he launched Winchester School on the unsuspecting and hitherto untroubled world. He did this in 1382 which makes Winchester the oldest Public School in the known universe and pooh-ie to all the rest, whatever they say. Incidentally, old Bill was also responsible for New College Oxford, so you can decide for yourself if he were hero or villain. I know what I think.

Well, in next to no time, Winchester was making

boffins out of barbers' sons and the dark ages saw the light. 'More schools for the serfs!' came the cry and the church, never slow to miss a marketing opportunity, obliged with enthusiasm. Shortly after that, schools became epidemic and all the best counties had one.

For a couple of hundred years, everything ticked along happily. The schools produced boring necessities like clerics, lawyers and obnoxious intellectuals and nobody paid them much mind. Then Francis Bacon, politician, essayist and perpetrator of the first Watergate scandal (*very* juicy for the court of James I) reared his cultured head and lobbed the *Advancement of Learning* at his fellow countrymen. The basic theory advanced in this amusing little tract is that anyone worth knowing can speak Latin and Greek (well, things always get worse before they get better) and anyone who can't is a yob, which is just the sort of thing you can expect from a precocious brat who went up to Cambridge at the age of 13. Next Milton happened out of St Pauls, told everyone how rotten they all were, paradise was lost and the whole caboose went haywire.

It was all very well, the rich felt, to have schools to provide people who could be bothered to read the small print, but when they started writing in blank verse, and got the backing of the nobility to boot, it was all a bit over the top. Much chin-pulling in the shires ensued, and the general opinion that Education is Important was printed in whatever the equivalent of the Daily Telegraph was then. No doubt it also occurred to proud fathers that having sons around who play stick the tail on the tutor with a lance had limited appeal and that things would be more tranquil without the little beasts at home, but if it did, history doesn't actually relate.

The schools responded to the increased demand with customary aplomb: they didn't mind educating gentrified numbskulls, they said, as long as the parents paid through the nose. Shortly after that the rot set in. These new boys, who weren't used to being nice to anyone, especially not paupers and vicars invented fagging for the former and mutinied against the latter who had actually dropped their dog-collars and were masquerading as teachers. In fact, things got so bad at one stage that the Master of Eton once opened his desk to find a Mastiff inside it. Before long, questions were being asked in the House, and there was a move to abolish Public Schools altogether for the safety of the nation.

All good things come to an end, however, even for the sons of the nobility, and by the time Tom Brown was being pi at Rugby, high jinks were out and the New Morality entered wearing hob-nailed boots. Everyone settled down to become endlessly dull pillars of society, which was just as well as Victoria was about to be crowned and ban amusement.

Thereafter it was all serious study and tons of team spirit and Public School. Anyone who was anyone continued to send their sons out of sheer force of habit; anyone who wished to become someone sent theirs out of right-minded ambition; and intelligent nobodies were still encouraged to keep the academic flags flying. Foreigners came too, usually because they fitted into all three categories in that oddly adaptable way that foreigners have.

Good. You are now more or less aware of the genesis of the modern Jenkins. If you feel the need to know any more there's an advanced reading list for swots attached.

On, on.

The Old Guard

. . . And Jenkins begat Jenkins and he had a son is what we're talking about here. In other words these are the boys who are at least the second generation to be educated at Public School.

Initially, as I have mentioned, they appear to be no different from their fellows, but a deeper investigation will prove that in subtle ways they are by no means the same. This should not lead you to make any foolhardy generalisations, though, for you should be learning by now that young Jenkins is one of the most determinedly contrary creatures under heaven.

The obvious place to start is with the incredibly arrogant minority. These are the chaps who are not only second generation Public School, but second generation at a *particular* Public School and are distinguished by their overwhelming assurance. Not for them the phobias of lesser mortals; they are already genned up on the institutional gobbledegook and therefore can understand the most complicated order thrown at them from day one. Thus they slip happily into school life without having to pause to wipe the egg off their faces, an exercise which, for the first term or so, is practically a daily one for the non-elite.

If the second generation Jenkinses suffer in any way it is at their own hands, the cause being a surfeit of pride which always precedes a fall. It usually happens like this: young Jenkins, umpteenth chip off the Old School block is told to do something.

'What?' he replies, ever a sticker for politesse.

'I said, go and get your muckins.'

'What?' repeats the boy, fearless of tiring his audience.

'Food, fathead!'

'Oh, you mean pickins,' laughs the pompous mite. 'I'd've thought you'd know that by now, considering how long you've been here. But then, your grandfather probably forgot to tell you. Or maybe he wasn't

Second generation at a particular public school

here?' he concludes sweetly, and prepares to exit on a wave of self-righteousness.

'I don't give a tuppeny toss about your grandfather, and we'll leave *mine* out of it, you little bleeder. Things have changed since your senile relative was here, thank god, and you just remember it!' Whereat the incensed elder boy delivers a hearty thwack on the child's ear as a kind of aide-memoire.

Needless to say, matters are rendered considerably worse if Jenkins is foolhardy enough to try this technique on a master and become almost irremediable if he deigns to correct the Principal. The boy may wonder what happened to the divine right of the Sussex Jenkinses when he first encounters this sort of treatment, but after the second or third dose he learns to contemplate his superiority in silence. Funnily enough, it is useless to try to pull social rank at Public School.

The biggest problem for the hereditary Jenkins, however, is trying to come to terms with the fact that nothing's for nothing in this world, as the platitude goes: this never used to be the case, he reasons, and can't for the life of him see why things have changed. Obviously this does not occur in all examples, but where it does, it is tantamount to a fatal flaw. The symptoms are a lackadaisical attitude to study, a penchant for skulduggery in sport and a passion for pranks. In later life he relies on Chums and Connections rather than advancement through personal effort. You will know him by his abhorrence of intellectuals, sloth in all things save the pursuit of pleasure, and a continuing mania for practical jokes which even gout cannot dim. If you see one old fogey with a walking frame trying to debag another in a similar state you can bet your bottom twenty pence piece it's an hereditary Jenkins.

Happily, his overwhelming assurance remains with

him throughout life. Yet there are times, when the wind changes or his wife votes Green, that a piquant shadow of bewilderment is reflected in his eyes: where did it all go, the feudal system?

The Men In The Middle

There are those who live in the middle mist, or so Rupert Brooke would have us believe, and if there is such a place it is undoubtedly inhabited by chaps whose fathers went to a *different* Public School. This type is worthy of much consideration, not to mention understanding and is quite easy to spot as he retains throughout his youth the air of one whom Scotty beamed up to the wrong place. While this particular specimen is under the microscope, girls, it is crucial to be aware that Public Schools are all about Tradition, the still centre of Time's Whirlpool, and any other purple metaphors you care to think of. Take this as your starting point, add a little mental agility, bung in a liberal dose of Jenkins-flavoured double-think (see Names chapter) and stir. Now you perceive why a boy who isn't an Old-whatever-his-father-is feels like a beached whale.

The problem is that when two almost equals are held up for comparison one gets the rosette and the other gets it in the neck. Course, there are those who claim to believe the two balance each other out, but really this is so much hog-wash: hand them a box of chocolates and you'll see what I mean; nothing will satisfy save, say, an orange creme, an orange whirl being just too beastly for words. So it is with Public Schools. The modern day greed for University Entrance Successes (as they are known) has pretty much evened out the better schools, but try telling Jenkins. Oh, and don't let's be reasonable. The relative merits of schools are the one thing the poor boy can safely be emotional about.

Actually, heightened academic standards are the single biggest reason for downward mobility on the Public School scale apart from father backing a duff syndicate at Lloyds and losing all his assets. Oh! ignominy. I mean, imagine it. All your life you've been down for the Old School and then the rotters get serious about the Common Entrance examination and bob's your uncle, Jenkins's destiny takes a nose dive. It's one thing to be expelled for unmentionable sins like smoking in the squash courts, but to be deprived of even that opportunity is just, well, bloody!

Furthermore, though papa may aim to be noble, especially if he knows he is a bantam-weight brain himself, somehow the regret just oozes through. The Old Boy* becomes furtive where once he was bluff, and mumbles when speaking to friends. Whenever other people mention their own highly successful brats he suffers an attack of whooping cough. Dismay is everywhere. The cause? Eventually he admits it to young Jenkins's godfathers: the boy won't be following in their corporate footsteps. He makes this confession guility sotto voce for he doesn't want to upset the Old Dear† (who can actually be deadlier than the male in disappointment) or, worse, his own father. It's because they brought the boy up on Noddy and Biggles, he tells them by way of excuse, as if trying to shift the blame to Big Ears and Ginger. But when they've finally drunk the whisky bottle dry, poor Mr Jenkins has to admit that it all boils down to the fact that the youngster had failed.

So the boy is banished to a lesser school where the

* 1: Jenkins for Dad
† 2: Jenkins for Mum

jargon is different and they don't even play the right games. Small wonder that he spends one half of his life hell-bent on success to make it all up to the family, and the other in abysmal despair because there seems little point in trying to make Captain of Soccer when papa only understands rugby.

The flip side of this particular coin is the Jenkins who is sent to a better Public School than his father. There can be all sorts of reasons for this, the worst of which is that Jenkins Jnr is a whole lot brighter than Jenkins Snr. This tends to imply (to the Old Boy at least) that the jumping genes come from the distaff side, which means the burden on his son is doubly great because he not only shares the suffering of his plummeting counterpart at the lesser school, but has to make sure his father doesn't feel threatened into the bargain. This means when he gets 47 grade ones at A-level he keeps quiet about it, whereas if he makes it into the tenth eleven he has the Old Boy killing fatted calves.

Obviously when you've suffered either of these sorts of angst in your schooldays the only way is up, which is why Middle Jenkins tends to make a go of things in his career – he finds the atmosphere in the boardroom of a multi-national conglomerate quite relaxing after what he's been through. He's fairly good news on the romance front too, having been forced to be perceptive from a tender age. But whatever you do, don't tell: it'll only worry him.

The Boys Jolly Nouveau

Should you discover that Jenkins hails from the Stockbroker Belt or Solihull it's a safe bet that his father was a Grammar School* Boy or an extremely

* Nearly obsolete form of state school almost obliterated in the early seventies on the grounds of ideological unsoundness, but now enjoying a freak reprise.

fly spiv. Unless he lets his address slip, though, you will probably muddle him up with the Middle Mist men described above. They all have the same kind of hunted air about them, poor dears.

The reason for Jenkins's tortured demeanour in this case is that he is not really very sure if he is fish or fowl, an uncertainty he could do without when he learns that during your first term at Public School you either sink or swim. Why? Well, it's all to do with Tradition again. (Dull, isn't it, this tradition thing?) School tradition dictates that the pursuit of riches is not on, probably because it is assumed that he has quite enough already. No, the acceptable thing is to be suave and violently amateurish about everything. I have often thought that this attitude more than any other separates the English man from his American cousin. History will no doubt decide which part of the family got it right, but for the time being, I think it's a blessing in disguise that we've got North Sea Oil.

Anyway, while he's away at school Jenkins slugs away manfully at subjects like sociology, since Latin is currently out of fashion as the essential non-essential knowledge to have, and he thinks he's doing splendidly. The thought of a career occasionally wings its dingy way across his unsullied mind, but he frightens it off with the time honoured incantation 'I think I might sit Oxbridge!'* Thus he is able to manifest an amateurish passion for learning and feels he is satisfying the demands of tradition wonderfully by being an academic kind of fish.

* This indicates that the boy is toying with the idea of sitting the entrance examinations for the Universities of Oxford and Cambridge. The charm of the idea used to lie in in the date of the examination, just before Christmas and a term after A-level. In other words it was a delaying tactic, nine times out of ten. Unfortunately the game's largely up on this one as the varsities got windy about losing people who were bright but couldn't afford the nine months off. Awfully worthy of the Governing Bodies but tough on Jenkins, as I'm sure you'll agree.

All this works superbly in term time, but it doesn't see him through the holidays. This is when he once again encounters the True Grit of his successful papa. Not unnaturally, the self-made Mr Jenkins awards A for effort and doesn't bother to grade amateurism at all, since he despises it. He wishes to see a Burning Urge in his offspring, and finding no light in his eyes indicative of that, he is apt to tap the child's backbone and find that lacking too. In next to no time he exposes his son's desire for the Dreaming Spires as mere flummery and asks what is the matter with the boy. Receiving no acceptable answer, he jumps on his favourite soap box and recites his well-known speech about the harshness of the world, the vicissitudes of the age, and the ogre of unemployment. This is supported by the odd well-chosen phrase indicating that he didn't get where he is today by virtue of a public school education – no, it was struggle, struggle for him which is why he's sent his son to Public School so that he should be free from all that and the least the boy could do is bloody well struggle a bit harder himself to show that he appreciates the sacrifices made on his behalf.

Confused? How do you think Jenkins feels when his father winds up asking what he has to say for himself?

By and large, the reply is 'Nothing'. Well, be fair, what would you say on spec? He can see his father's point of view, of course, and even accepts the validity of certain points. It would help if these points weren't in direct conflict with those made by the school, however. The beleagured boy shakes his head to make the knotted hotchpotch of his thoughts settle into a more sensible order. The attempt is a failure. He gives up the academic fish notion for the rest of the holiday, and just feels foul instead.

Still, there is no such thing as a bad experience, or

so people would have one believe. Conflict in the cul-de-sacs of the soul is character building. The benefit of the brou-ha-ha described above is that the Nouveau Jenkins is taught from an early age to see more sides to an issue than there are angles to the Sydney Opera House. Obviously, this deters him from making snap decisions, and if you don't believe me try asking how he'd like his eggs cooked in the morning: it'll probably be suppertime before he chooses. On the other hand he develops an endearing safety valve: he tends to see the funny side of every problem. This can make him slightly cynical, but he usually manages to turn this to his own advantage and everyone else's amusement.

Sometimes, however, he just turns into a paranoid schizophrenic. But that sort of thing can happen to anyone, you know.

The Show Case

Every school has a show case: the exhibits usually inhabit one particular House* and are known collectively as 'Scholars' or something like that. These are the boys who keep the academic aspidistra from wilting and were originally blue-printed by William of Wykeham (cf. potted history above).

Nowadays Scholars are not necessarily poor. They are, however, always dangerously close to genius, and often more than a little strange. In fact the ones that I've met are so clever and so odd that I have hardly dared speak to them so I wouldn't presume to write about them. They're probably really nice and normal, though. I mean, don't let me put you off. Life with a mastermind is awfully, well, stimulating, I imagine.

* House = building where boys eat and sleep. The word could be synonymous with 'tribe'. It has absolutely nothing to do with home.

Most Of The Rest Of The World

The modern Jenkins comes in all shapes and shades. The genealogy of the non-caucasian sector is more or less the History of Everywhere, and if you think you're going to run into that here, I'll take it as a back-handed compliment. You won't though, you know. I'm still waiting to see the movie.

In the meantime, here's a brief synopsis. To put it simply, the rest of the world started to come to Public School when Britannia started to have an empire. The empire didn't have a lot of staying power, but the Foreign Public Schoolboy did. Their presence has encouraged détente on the sporting fields of the world and it seems to me if only all the sides would play as fair when they grew up to be international politicians the planet would be a lot less messy.

Isn't naïveté wonderful?

Sorry. I'll get back to reality right now.

The Final Pieces Of The Jigsaw

Many Public Schools now admit women to the 6th form at least. These girls are a catalyst in the whole system and their presence will doubtless have a lasting, civilising influence.

In fact I am sure that eventually their observations will supersede, if not obviate, my own. However, from the close consultation I have had with several of these ladies I gather the long term effect of their presence is, as yet, unquantifiable. So all I can do is applaud their amazing fortitude, wish them buckets of luck and hope that they will understand that though they are very much 'members of the class', in a guide to the English Public School*boy* they can only make a guest appearance.

Brothers Under The Skin

The wonderful thing about Public Schoolboys, as I intimated in the introduction to this chapter, is that regardless of class, race, colour or creed, after a couple of terms at school it is very hard to tell them apart. All *sorts* of people go to public school nowadays darling, it's true, but at least none of them lower the tone. The end result is, as it ever was, a stickler for convention and tradition who is in every way a 'verray parfit gentel knight' with a few mischievously rough edges.

Now, this may be cause for celebration for you and me but it doesn't afford Jenkins nearly the same sense of ease. He will insist on trying to fool the outsider into believing that he is not what he is, if you follow me. These days the fashionable closet Jenkins hides behind ninety ill-fitting second-hand suits from jumble sales, and drops as many aitches as he can without devolving to total incoherence. There are those pundits who explain this as the boy's way of expressing solidarity with the victims of the economic recession and I am sure that there is some truth in this. I would also contend that pretty though the theory be, it is not the whole truth: if there is one thing Jenkins cannot stand, it's standing out from the crowd; it embarrasses him. Of which more later.

Test

Tick the applicable box

1. Do you know where your Jenkins's father went to school?
   Yes. No. Can't quite remember.
2. Do you mind?
   Yes. No.

3. Do you know what his father does?
   Yes. No. Can't quite remember.

4. Does this worry you?
   Yes. No.

5. Do you know what Jenkins's views on education are?
   Yes. No. Can't quite remember.

6. Do you wish they were different?
   Yes. No. Couldn't care less.

7. Does any of this matter?
   Yes. No. Don't know.

Scores

1. Yes= 2; No = 0; C.Q.R = 1
2. Yes = 0; No = 1
3. Yes = 2; No = 0; C.Q.R. = 1
4. Yes = 0; No = 1
5. Yes = 0; No = 2; C.Q.R. = 1
6. Yes = 1; No = 2; Don't care = 0
7. Yes = 1; No = 2; Don't know = 1

Results

0–4 Are you *sure* you know what you're doing?
5–8 Balanced female, should go far.
9–12 Blind adoration never got anyone anywhere.

Health and Hygiene

Ideally, great romance should involve the marriage of like minds and all that high fallutin' stuff, and have very little to do with physical attributes. Realistically, few would deny that physical attraction plays at least some part in getting the whole affair off the ground in the first place, and physical habits are quite influential when the thrill of flight is beginning to wear off. Even the most besotted of girls rather prefers her man to come housetrained, unless of course she takes it for granted that he will be. If you fall into this category you have much to learn. Brace yourself.

Cleanliness Is Next To Cissyness

Though Jenkins, in common with other little boys, is not made from slugs and snails and puppy dogs' tails, you could be forgiven for thinking that the old nursery rhyme was written for him by an embittered nanny. Throughout his youth, his complexion is sluggish, his fingernails indicate a passion for helping the lowly worm aerate the good earth, and at this stage his aroma is reminiscent of puppies. Untrained puppies.

Apparently the boy is either allergic to soap and water or ignorant of their powers. However, unpleasant though the manifestations of this sorry state may be they are *entirely* understandable. Think about it logically, and you will soon find yourself more

Cleanliness is next to cissyness

sympathetic to him if not entirely converted to his way of thinking.

At Prep school, the only person who wields loofahs, looks behind ears and generally insists on the removal of personal grime is Matron. Housemasters are so busy planning Matches and the like that they manifest a reckless lack of concern about the invertebrates their charges are nurturing in their navels.

At home, Jenkins's health and bodily welfare are the burden of the female members of the family, who resort to espionage-agent-techniques to induce the boy to bathe ocassionally. They tell of film stars who spend every spare second in the jacuzzi and point out that even boxers shower now and then. At Christmas they donate gift-wrapped hints like Soap On A Chain for the Really Masculine Man and tell him in excitingly low tones that clean skin is a turn-on for girls.

These ploys, so carefully thought out, seldom work, as for most of his life and all of his childhood Jenkins thinks film stars are queer, boxers thick and girls about as interesting as yesterday's porridge. Meanwhile, the menfolk of the household rain wonderful presents on the lad – things like fancy rats, Swiss army knives and eventually the Kama Sutra in plain bindings. It's terribly unfair of them but when challenged they just pose around aloofly, and observe that the child will learn by example; they might back this limp argument by saying that he seems to be very competent at using a loo correctly. It is no good attacking with a tart remark about it being precisely their example that the boy should *not* follow, especially if you happen to be the mother, as this can lead to tedious discussions about why you got married in the first place, and, if not controlled, can end in divorce.

All this means that young Jenkins grows up with the erroneous impression that everything to do with hygiene has apron strings attached and is therefore cissy. As you will by now be beginning to realise, anything that is even ever so faintly cissy is avoided like the plague, because it is only one step away from the spectre of homosexuality, and before much longer I dare say that you, in common with the rest of us, will want to throttle the next person to use the term. OK, OK, men should be manly and all that, but does it *have* to be Neanderthal man every time?

Of course, if you are feeling particularly indulgent towards the boy, you can make excuses for him. It can't be much fun having to wash in public: there are times when one needs space to contemplate the nether regions in privacy. The mere thought of communal wash-rooms certainly turns my stomach, what with all those unclaimed hairs and so on that you find in the youth hostels of Europe.

On the other hand, don't spend too much time fretting about any barbaric conditions your man may have had to endure, since you can bet *he* wouldn't have changed them for the world. Not so long ago, one of our more hallowed institutions held a referendum to see if the boys would like to join the rest of us in the 20th century and have hot water to bathe in instead of having to chip their way through the ice to the cleansing pools beneath. With lemming like unanimity they answered in the negative. They had grown used to cold baths they said and anyway they were too old to cope with change now. Goodness knows how they will adapt to the everyday advances that the rest of us have to take in our stride. They will probably grow up to be Luddites.

For God, Harry And St Jude

Having made all these rash generalisations, I suppose I ought to qualify them, because there *is* nothing so determinedly awkward as a Jenkins. As with everything else, his policy on cleanliness is far from consistent. In fact, though it is cavalier to say the least, when he is abroad, Cromwell himself would find no cause for complaint. For Jenkins, when extricated from his normal environment is quite the staunchest supporter of the bath. When he is staying with friends he dips with tepid enthusiasm and when overseas he ablutes with a verve that is almost unhealthy and certainly does not help his relationship with drought-afflicted natives. The reason for this turnabout has taxed greater minds than mine for some considerable time, and it distresses me to have to report that the know-alls have come to no satisfactory conclusion to date. So you'll have to make do with mine.

It appears likely that this mania for jumping from tub to tub in the far flung corners of what used to be the colonies is a curious form of flag-waving. Throughout his school career Jenkins is trained to believe that his role in life is to lead by example, to inspire lesser mortals to greater heights through emulation. Somewhere in his heart of hearts he knows that cleanliness is a Good Thing and though he may not know why, he is conditioned to transmit his superior knowledge.

Another aspect of the whole thing is one that would easily be understood by trade unionists. It is a little matter of differentials. The only thing that makes the Brits different and altogether better than anyone else is that Others are known to be dirty and we are not. Thus, Jenkins's obsession with setting the standard could be attributed to a desire to remind them that this is not the homeland of the Mother of Parliaments for nothing.

Perhaps the most pressing reason, however, relates to the chap's fervent hypochondria. Jenkins is usually the world's worst invalid, and unless he has the world's best nurses (mummy and nanny, preferably) he is reluctant to succumb. Added to this is his conviction that nowhere but in one's own home can one trust the environment, and you will find good enough excuses for the most hardened Jenkins to spend half his waking life in baths other than his own.

Puberty Blues

Though Jenkins's body is a problem throughout life, it reaches a particular crisis point at puberty. So what, you might say, it's the same for the rest of us? You only have to pick up a Sunday newspaper to know that. What makes Jenkins so different? Not a lot, really, if you are going to be relentlessly rational about things. But do remember that relentless rationale is about as common in Jenkins as myxomatosis. His breakthrough to manhood is an out and out trauma, and if you thought that learning to cope with the curse and a chest expanding like Russia was bad enough, you can rest assured that Jenkins was having a worse time of it than you can ever ever dream of, Horatia.

In many ways this will not shock you if you have ever met any perfectly normal men. Even the most sheltered of girls must have noticed how the majority of the opposite sex book a cab to the morgue when they have a slight cough. It appears that the male biorhythm is more volatile than the female equivalent and tolerance to pain, except when fighting the Hun or playing rugger, is zilch.

Needless to state Jenkins, bless him, takes this to its logical extreme. For some reason he believes that frailty's alias is woman, despite all evidence to the contrary and so concludes that minor ailments are cissy, and the only ones you dare admit to are major ones.

Thus he will pretend that a mere cold is pleural

pneumonia; and by the same token approaches puberty as though it were a serious, if not terminal, illness. Which in turn explains why many a lass has tried to force her brother to read *Little Women*. Poor Beth didn't complain, they point out, not even when her little needle was too heavy for her tiny hand to hold. Which is just a polite way of telling Jenkins to shut up about his various growing pains.

It is easy to deduce from this that a Public School-boy knows how to suffer, but is opposed to doing so in silence. This is particularly noticeable in later life when the man has a hangover. He just won't accept that to shout at the cat for walking too loudly, will only make things worse.

This is part of his tendency always to disregard scientific findings when it suits him – a tendancy all too obvious in puberty. It is just a waste of breath to advise him that things can't be rushed. Someone once told him that your voice will drop if you yodel loud enough from the top of an alp and he believes it. Thus many a poor Swiss has been confounded by the vision of several lusty young men belting out *Jerusalem* for all they are worth. No wonder they think the English are mad.

Of course, the on-going-adolescent situation is not helped by a certain element of competition. There is a dubious honour in being the first one to muck-up a recital of 'Oh for the wings of a dove' and even more in being the first to shave. At a certain point it becomes unbearable *not* to have to shave. One Jenkins known to me was so mortified by his lack of bristles that he took to shaving with an unloaded razor. For months he creamed the shaving foam across his silky jaws and splashed it off again undetected. Then one fateful morn a friend asked to borrow his razor. Jenkins prevaricated to no avail. His guilty secret was out. 'I say, there's no blade in

Jenkins razor. Guffaw guffaw.' The loss of face hasn't been regained to this day.

Of course when he really does need to shave, he will refuse to do so, thus causing great discomfort to the recipient of his passionate if pungent kisses. He just will not accept that a 10 day shadow is about as appealing to tender female flesh as a quick tumble with a rasp: he thinks it rather macho.

Oh, yes, before I forget, a brief word about the pack ethic illustrated above. It isn't all dog eat dog. In fact to an outside observer it would appear that all are united. So if you are the first girl to infiltrate beware the snapping of jaws at your feet: the others don't want to break up the happy band. Conversely, if all the hounds but one has his mate, cave! The rest will unite to ensnare you for their love-lorn comrade. If this makes you feel you can't win, brace up: no-one said you had to fight fair!

Still, it would be mean to be too scathing about Jenkins's puberty blues: it can't be easy to go through all the usual traumas under the scrutiny of so many others. On the other hand, it is possible to be too understanding. It was recently suggested to me that when a boy is ill he gets to see Matron and therefore some much needed attention, which is why he exaggerates the whole puberty thing so much. This sounds a little bit like biased rationalisation to me, especially when one remembers that matrons and the like are generally more to be feared than sought out, these worthy women being well able to spot a shammer when they see one. Anyway, even if it is true, it should be discouraged. Most Jenkinses expect far too much cossetting as it is!

Out Damned Spot

One of the most upsetting attributes of puberty is acne, at least for girls. The same is not true for

Jenkins. After all the other moans and groans you'd expect spots to inspire suicidal tendencies, but not a bit of it.

Take my own brother, for example. He positively cultivated a crop of the things. Mummy and I were mortified. His features, hitherto cherubic, were ringed by a halo of positively dangerous looking eruptions. Anyone would have thought he was an orphan or something. But it wasn't the spots that were the real cause of the pain, it was hardly his fault if he looked like a currant pudding – no, it was the obvious pleasure that he took in them that got us down. In vain we'd say things like 'they'll only get worse if you eat chocolate and chips dear' while offers of astringents and other spot killing potions were treated as slights on his good name. In fact anything we said seemed to underline the fact that men and women come from different galaxies.

The point being, that to Jenkins, a really pustulent plook is worth preserving. It proves to the peer group at school that he is growing up apace and will soon be shaving (cf. above). But I ask you, what kind of status symbol is this?

It should be said that not all Jenkinses go through such ecstasies about their nasties and some will tell you that a polka-dot fizog was far from their idea of bliss. *They* suffered, by God! They laid siege to the local chemist and purchased any number of foul-sounding creams which never cleared their complexions but turned them green instead! These are the sorts of chap who will wax nostalgic about zit popping sessions in the bathroom and mourn that the only pleasure in front of the mirror these days is checking that the tooth decay is coming along nicely.

Ah, but can we believe them? A friend of mine, discovering her 14-year-old brother in tears, asked what was wrong – it had to be something drastic, she thought, if he was actually blubbing, since Jenkins regards this as the next worse thing to kissing in public. Between sobs she was told that Jenkins Ma. a blot of 16, had mocked him for his baby-faced looks. He's jealous, consoled Elizabeth, only to be told that that wasn't the point. He wanted spots like everyone else. It was crucial.

Slightly at a loss, Elizabeth told him she thought you could buy spots in joke shops if desperate, and left him to his own devices. Suffice it to say that the next day after a trip to town, the child bore the marks of the most awful dermatitis in history.

Sad to reflect this wrongheadedness about the physical manifestations of the Inner Man continues further into adulthood. One example being a Jenkins I used to work with who would have been quite the most delicious thing on two legs had it not been for the thing that he proudly kept atop these lush limbs: a beer paunch. It was useless to tell him that it was only this vast tummy that kept him from instant global recognition as a sex symbol, and that the entire typing pool might be his if he would just dispense with his lamentable spare barrel. He liked his paunch, that was the problem. He had been considered a weed at school and now his stomach was instant proof to the most casual of observers that he was a weed no more but One Of The Boys. It made him feel better, it comforted him. And I guess if that was all he wanted, it was a less degrading way of getting there than carrying a security blanket around at the ripe old age of thirty.

The Unbalanced Diet

Fortunately, pimples are a passing affliction and sooner or later they go out of fashion with the chaps at school. This usually coincides with the onset of a noticeable weirdness at about the age of sixteen – a phase commonly known as The Revolting Stage (see chapter of that name). I can tell you that Jenkins's dietary requirements at that stage have caused sous-chefs to go well and truly under by now, and have turned culinary masters anorectic.

Fortunally, the food fads are short-lived, Jenkins's tum, and more importantly his bowel, soon dictate that he should stick to basics: meat, spuds and spotted dick. It is trying to have to add that though his tastes change, his attitudes seldom differ; and when it comes to attitudes, Jenkins is an absolute whizz. The older version of the species is apt to rhapsodise about Les Vins Fins and Les Banquets he has known, but this is no more than a ruse and you shouldn't be taken in by it. Despite all he says, Jenkins is no gourmet. When the chips are down you will find that as far as he is concerned, food is simply fuel. Lingering lunches are not on the menu, as you will soon discover, unless of course they are largely liquid.

A secretary friend of mine was silly enough to accept at face value her film director boss's claims to epicureanism. The poor lamb just didn't notice that despite a thin veneer of trendy sophistication, the man was really a Jenkins to the core. Thus when he complained that the food in the studio where they were working was repellant she listened. When he clutched his belly and said another plate of pie and beans would make him into an anarchist she trembled. When he said he would give his sponsor for a steak tartare and asparagus she made a note of it.

The next day she went to great lengths to procure the dreamed of repast and presented it proudly, waiting for the praise due to a girl who has saved a chap from the grisly fate of becoming an anarchist. Poor thing. All she got was a disgusted yelp followed by 'Whaddaya mean by giving me raw meat and phallic symbols? This is a bloody studio not a harem, you know'. If I'd been in her shoes the studio certainly would have been bloody, and the asparagus would have been up his nostrils. But Claire is the resilient sort and said she would find him something more sustaining.

Moments later he was happily chomping on 'Boeuf et champignons en croute avec les haricots et pommes frites' which just shows what you can do with beef and mushroom pie, beans and chips from the canteen. It also demonstrates a greal deal about Jenkins's attitude to the finer things in life.

Natural Rhythm

Whatever pains you might endure trying to understand his diets and general personal habits, you will never have to puzzle over the condition of Jenkins's bowels. You will know all about them. You will know because you will be told. And if you aren't told in words, you will be given clues.

That early morning trumpet you never used to hear, followed by an unmistakable odour, is in fact the common fart. It is nothing to worry about, still less cause for complaint; it's just Jenkins saying 'hello how are you' to one of his most beloved parts. The reason for this unusual affection is something to do with the precision timing which is impressed upon a chap at school. One Prep, favoured by fathers for the pristine state of its lavatories, has people who conduct a sort of Spanish inquisition on the boys every morning. Matron, or one of her acolytes demands to know if the child is a yes, a no or a question mark. If there is doubt Jenkins is cross-questioned and a liberal dose of Cod Liver Oil or Kaolin and Morphine is administered post-haste to rectify the situation right speedily. As the new female force in Jenkins's life you would be well advised to listen to his morning litanies with a sympathetic ear and have bottles of CLO and K & M tucked safely behind your moisturiser.

Incidentally, once you work out the time that your man goes off to do his duty for King and Country in the loo, you would be wise to plan your own requirements accordingly as he will not take kindly to being interrupted. You will notice that he marches purposefully forth with the Sunday papers or a couple of volumes of Dostoevsky tucked under his arm: he's going to enjoy himself in there and you had better believe it.

It might seem odd to some, this pursuit of happiness in the lavatory, but once again, to understand is to sympathise. Public schools by definition are not very private places and certainly some of the older ones offer about as much seclusion as Waterloo Station in the rush hour. In fact, the only time a boy finds himself alone with his inner soul is behind the khazi door. The hunted feeling never leaves him, even though he might end up living in a mansion with twenty private studies and forty footmen to keep the world at bay. Oh, and should you find yourself in such a place, don't think you can relax. There might be more loos than there are dinner plates but Sods' Law dictates that whichever one you pick will be the thunder box of the day for your lord and master as well. I need hardly tell you who will have to give up her seat.

The most important thing to learn about Jenkins's bowels is that they are a sort of secondary nervous system, and as such must be accorded due reverence. You must never grow bored by hearing about them. Remember that Jenkins has been brought up on horror stories about head-boys who fell from grace because they refused to swallow matron's bitter remedies, and of brave men who lost all because their bowels were out of sync. Witness the experience of one chap who, in common with the rest of his year, was subject to a talk before he left his Prep school. He knew that what he was about to hear had been designed to provide him with a set of guidelines for the future, so he listened attentively. He heard the following masterpiece of English rhetoric, which was delivered by an Old Boy of the school.

'And remember boys, wherever you are, whatever you may do, make sure that you *go regularly*. When you're in the trenches the Bosch won't stop the bally battle to let you go then, so make sure you get it over with early in the morning. Then you'll never be one of those silly arses caught in no-man's land with your trousers down.'

The year was 1963.

With this sort of example to follow, it shouldn't surprise you that Jenkins takes great care to ensure that his body goes like clockwork. It should also be a great solace. For when all seems lost, when you can't seem to make him understand that deodorant has its advantages and that toothbrushes aren't specifically designed for cleaning the trickier bits of a motor bike, you have one certain knowledge to cling to: in Jenkins you have a truly regular boyfriend.

Test: Can You Really Look After Him?

1. Does your medicine cabinet contain
   a) K & M b) CLO c) A choice of three headache cures d) a supply of dramatic looking bandages for when the cat scratches him?

2. Think of six alternative ways of describing pie and chips (e.g. boeuf et champignons en croute avec les pommes de terres, etc., etc.)

3. Describe the workings of the digestive system.

Scores

Q.1. Score a point for each tick.
Q.2. Score a point for each tick.
Q.3. Score nil. Whatever you've said, I bet you're bluffing.

9 or more is a pass. Are you a member of the WRVS or are you just a hypochrondriac yourself?
8 or less is a fail. You'll never muster enough sympathy, dear.

Judging by Appearances

There is nothing quite so indicative of a man's background as his appearance, and in no man is this quite so true as in the Public Schoolboy. By and large, when he has grown out of his various phases, he sports reasonably expensive clothes – clothes which would look lovely on anyone else, but don't do much for him. It's as though he liked his outfitter well enough to buy clothes from the man but not enough to listen to his advice on how to wear the damn things. You've guessed, haven't you – sartorial elegance, like personal hygiene, is not one of Jenkins Min's stronger points.

This is largely because in his youth he knew exactly what to wear and when. At school there was one uniform, and at home there was more or less another. Term time apparel was dictated by tradition; mufti was handled by mummy.

The Uniform Approach

From a very early age, Jenkins has been led to believe that wearing the correct uniform was almost as important as keeping his bowels open. So once he had learned how to put the various garments on in the correct order, dressing became more of a habit than anything else. Thence was born the conviction that what you looked like with your clothes on was as much an Act of God as what you looked like with them off, and therefore not worth bothering about. This erroneous impression tends to last, much to the chagrin of wives and girlfriends.

One of the most important things about dressing, as with all other things at school, was timing. A boy had to be properly covered before he was allowed to get to grips with his cornflakes of a morning, and so a Jenkins can usually go from naked ape to fully clothed scarecrow in seventy-five seconds flat.

The Rite Of Eventide

Because of the precision timing required at school, Jenkins has the whole process of dressing down to a fine art, though you may not think so from looking at him. This involves a great deal of forethought which, over the years, has developed into a ritual truly beautiful to behold. As the whole exercise is determined by the expected time of waking it does not occur at the weekend when Jenkins's behaviour is leisurely to say the least. This means that the Dressing Rite can only be seen from Sunday to Thursday nights inclusive. Oh yes . . . in case you hadn't realised, it happens at night to alleviate the pain of preparation in the morning.

For some reason the laying out of the clothes begins with the footwear and works upwards. The shoes are the first items to be put in the correct place. They are seldom polished all over, unless Jenkins has strong military blood in him or he is expecting to see his bank manager on the morrow.

By and large only the toes and heels are treated to a quick spit and dust at the best of times. Apparently special care is taken over the heels because legend has it that a chap was once blackballed from a club because the backs of his shoes were filthy. Hardly anyone belongs to a club any more, partly because there are hardly any clubs left, so one would have thought that most attention would be paid to the toes these days. This is not the case. As has been noted before, Jenkins is a traditionalist and old habits die hard.

By each shoe a sock is placed, then the trousers are thrown over a convenient chair or something. Great care is taken to ensure that the trouser legs are pointing towards the socks – in case he forgets what to do with his feet in the morning, I suppose. Or maybe it's because the older Jenkins frequently wakes up with a 14-megaton hangover, cannot take the sunlight and has to feel his way to his shoes in the dark. Anyhow, once the trousers are in regimental position, he flings a pair of knickers on top in a nonchalant kind of fashion.

Having got this far, Jenkins will steel himself for the most complicated part of the ritual. Regardless of what he is wearing at the time, he will put on the chosen shirt for the next day and then add the jacket. Following that he takes both off again, the knack being to leave the sleeves of the shirt inside those of the jacket so that the two can be put on as one in the morning. Fortunately waistcoats are seldom worn, so there is no problem with gravity mucking up the whole thing by pulling the waistcoat down, the sleeves out and so on and so forth.

After that there is only the tie to worry about, and this is put within easy stretching distance. Needless to state, this item has not been properly untied since Creation and so sits there like a very greasy used noose. I find the sight of it rather sinister and try not to look.

Nothing in the above outfit will necessarily be clean, nor in good repair. Also, one should always be deeply suspicious of a Jenkins wearing a tie-pin, especially if it is stuck at an odd angle. It usually means that he has something to hide like an old wine stain or traces of baked bean. This is the sort of chap who holds up the hem of his jacket with masking tape and staples his shirt cuffs together. He is to be avoided, since should he decide you are the woman for him your entire life will be spent mending and washing for him and, if you show remotely willing, for all his bachelor friends as well.

The Importance Of Looking Right

This is another of those relatively serious bits, but happily less of a yawn than the last one because it is of material interest to anyone aspiring to the position of being Jenkins's personal valet. So pay attention.

If you are brought up properly (i.e. as a Jenkins) you know that there is a correct way of dressing for every occasion. This is lovely, for two reasons. First it means you don't have any decisions to make. Fair enough, if you want to flaunt your flair you can have a couple of extra ruffles on your dress shirt or something, but the basics remain the same. Rather convenient this, when you think about it – no worries about going strapless or backless for him, no panics about being too prim or too risqué, just the calm security of a uniform. And to make doubly sure he does not get confused, formal invitations tell him what to wear in neat embossed print. I have sometimes wondered if this is not yet another manifestation of devious sexism – I mean, no-one tells us girls, do they? But I digress.

The second benefit falls into two parts: prescribed apparel means a) that Jenkins knows that he won't stand out in a crowd and be embarrassed; and b) that if the crowd is a big, mixed one he can easily locate his own tribe because they are all in national costume.

Two sides of the same coin, you may cry. Absolutely right. It's all part of recognising who is who. The Freemasons are more subtle about it, but in a way, Jenkins's dress is as significant as a secret handshake.

The subtlety for him lies in the way various garments are worn. Apparently you can tell a man's name, rank and number, or rather school and era, from the way he folds his hanky, and such like. For instance, anyone who was anyone at Wellington before the Great War used to wear his cap in a fashion that defied gravity and despised anyone who covered his head with the thing instead. Unfortunately I can't shed any more light on this particular ethic; even Jenkins can play some things close to his chest. I put it down to self preservation.

Needless to state it was all much easier for us girls in the Old Days. You know, the rosy past when everything was better except living standards, sanitation and health care. It was easier still during any period after the time when men wore trousers as opposed to those silly bell-like tutus favoured by Henry VIII & Co.

Those were the days when everyone had his place, knew it, and was expected to show that he knew it. Even the gentry had to show its true colours, much to its chagrin. Thus you judged a man's Prospects at a glance; Number One Son could wear anything expensive because he was destined to be a gentleman; Number Two Son flounced around in military apparel because that was the next best thing and anyhow big bro' might fall off his phaeton before the Old Boy; and Number Three donned a dog-collar because his rewards had to be in heaven, since they certainly wouldn't come down here. This made life a lot easier for fortune hunting mammas, for they could tell immediately who was on the reject pile and was a proof of honesty also for those who married for love:

after all, if you married a soldier or vicar there could be no other reasonable excuse!

Things have changed quite a bit since then, as you may be aware. I think this is a great step forward and adds to the excitement: you never quite know what you're letting yourself in for. But then I always was an incurable romantic and used to be an optimist as well!

There is, I think, a hint of exhibitionism in the shrinkingest of violets, and at one stage or another, most of us let it out, even if only to the extent of wearing purple mascara. The traditional time for self-parody is the mid-teens, but for those few souls trapped between matron and the school rules this is not allowed. Then it happens later in life, more obviously and, praise be, is short-lived. Still, it has a certain oblique charm while it lasts.

It is only when he is free from the constraints of school that Jenkins gets his big break and can bring personal taste to the fore. He usually celebrates this wonderful liberation by flinging together a riotous assembly of hues which have been at loggerheads since time began. Even the knickers may be day-glo, or worse, have Union Jacks on them. In short Jenkins in the peacock stage is probably the sole reason that ladies wear dark glasses in Belgravia. At this stage he may well wear a red velvet jacket to a black tie dinner and even flaunt propriety so far as to flash yellow wellies in the country.

All too soon, however, he is made to understand that play time is no time to show just how colourful he can be if he chooses. If he is a shooting man he is swiftly informed that if he continues to dress like a hoopoe he will no longer be invited to kill pheasant, but be drummed out of the counties instead. If he retaliates by saying that he doesn't care – he was planning to join the Royal Society for the Protection of Birds anyhow, he will be thrown out of his club and disinherited, and will soon come around to seeing the merit of annihilating fowls and dressing quietly. Similar sanctions are brought to bear on the subjects of evening, party and sports wear, so that quite soon Jenkins finds himself the soberest of poseurs.

The final death knell for his peacock self, rung when he gets a job, at which point he finds that he has to wear another sort of uniform, is a mere caprice of fate. Thereafter, apart from occasionally wearing a checked shirt with a pin-striped suit he ceases to cause headaches in all who survey him. The only way that you will ever see how this curbing of individuality has grated on his soul will be to look at his socks: the one on the right foot seldom started life paired with the one on the left.

Best Dress

It would be unkind and unjust to say that every Jenkins under the English Heaven is oblivious to his appearance: there are some who try very hard. It should also be pointed out that one reason that they are all so shy of looking their best is the fear that when he does make an effort his friends will cry 'Fop'! And when they do try, the effect can be devastating, because as I mentioned they don't usually buy clothes which are truly awful in their own right

On high days and holidays, however, even the scruffiest of Jenkins Mins will make some concessions to public decency and a sprucing up operation will be deemed in order. This will be achieved to his own full satisfaction by ironing the front two wings of the shirt, or at least the bits that show. If a woman is available things change somewhat, and a fully ironed shirt is required daily.

The time when *all* Public Schoolboys come into

their own is a formal occasion. Whenever there is a wedding or a formal ball or something of that ilk the man seems to transcend the lesser self and acquire a certain dignity which is absolutely staggering. This is usually because his tails and morning coat and so forth have been handed down from his grandfather, and the weight of the family honour sits heavy upon his shoulders. At such times he should be complimented at regular five minute intervals with comments like 'You do look good when you stand up straight. Tell me, were you always an admirer of Quasimodo or is it just that life had been getting you down since we met?' and one day you might persuade him to drop the Public School stoop. But even when they are attempting to outdo Beau Brummel himself, they do advertise their Jenkinsdom by two little tell tale signs. No Public Schoolboy wears his trousers very tight, it would be considered obscene at least and a confession of guilt at most. Anyway, there has to be enough slack to accommodate the beer paunch at its greatest extent. So the back flap of the shirt tends to excape and can generally be seen peeping shyly out from under the sweater, or just wafting gently in the breeze. In his youth, Jenkins often used this material as a blotter and it was frequently ink-stained. Experience gradually teaches him that there are better things to use for this than his shirt flap, so by the time you first spot this signal it should be fairly clean. Its role as mopper-upper has been overtaken by the handkerchief, which is the second piece of silent Jenkins semaphore, and can usually be seen hanging from the back pocket like a grubby flag of truce. Both are oddly endearing and likely to bring out your motherly instincts. The two together are also the dead giveaway that the wearer is a Jenkins.

I had a Latin teacher once who was forever exhorting me to 'spectate caudam, puella!' Now, at last, I realise what she was on about.

The Essential Garment

By now it should come as no surprise to discover that the one item of clothing in which Jenkins consistently shows interest is his knickers. Research shows that these are frequently of the cut-off pantomime variety and thus quite likely to make you giggle helplessly, which is something to avoid if you possibly can because, being a sensitive flower, Jenkins can find this mirth hurtful. But when they get to the fluted stage and resemble nothing so much as a tiny frilly petticoat which somehow fails to conceal any of the important bits, you are a far nicer girl than I am if you can keep a straight face.

In all seriousness, this type of knicker was chosen with good reason. First, I am told, it is more comfortable. Secondly there is a tale which has been handed down the generations that one Jenkins was called to his father's death-bed to hear the following immortal last words: 'And son, never wear y-fronts, or you could be the last in the line which would break your great-grandsire's heart'. Enigmatic to you and me maybe, but it seems to have struck a vital chord with Jenkins.

Washing Instructions

When you take up your post as chief laundress you may well discover that some of the garments in Jenkins's wardrobe don't really belong to him at all, a fact betrayed by the name tapes so carefully stitched into the hem. This is particularly true of socks.

Do not be alarmed. Jenkins is not really a kleptomaniac and the interlopers have all been with him since his days of fighting in the changing rooms. Quite what he was fighting about, or why a sock is proof of victory you may never know and frankly, I wouldn't ask.

Whatever you do, don't offer to return them to their rightful owner when he drops round for a drink. This is not the done thing. To Jenkins these holey, smelly rags are the spoils of internecine war and it's not your place casually to proclaim armistice just because you can't bear the shame of taking the things to the laundry one more time.

It's a sort of love-me-love-my-socks thing. Learn to live with them: they'll be the least of your domestic worries.

Homework

Learn how to tie a bow tie – a must for every girl.

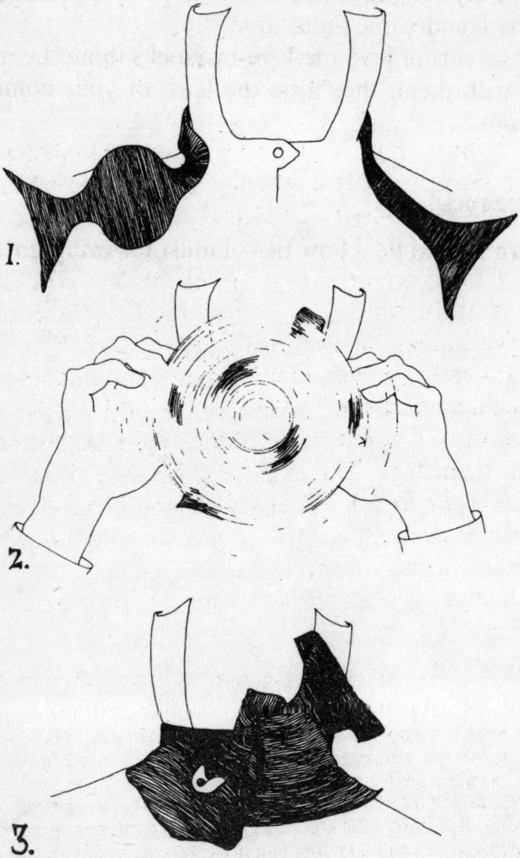

Bow-tie instructions!

Ich Dien – Or Rather You Do

Next time you have nothing to do in Manhattan, nab the nearest native and challenge him to a round of Tennis-elbow-foot. Explain the rules if necessary* then open play by saying 'Public School'. Ten to one he'll say Eton, tie or fagging. The point of the exercise is to learn which parts of the system have had the biggest press, internationally.

It's rather galling really, when you think about it. I mean, about a third of the New World seems to think that the old world is still trafficking in slaves, only we call them fags. This is largely because they have all read *Tom Brown's Schooldays* and believed it. Still, from a nation that still thinks London is swamped nightly in pea-soupers, you can't expect a lot.

Sadly, there is little I can do to correct these

* This is how to explain the rules of Tennis-elbow-foot to an American:

'Tennis-elbow-foot is a socio-educational activity designed to stimulate the powers of self expression via association. One guy says a word, see, and the next guy has to relate to it by giving a similar sort of word. Right? If he can't relate the relationship to the first guy, he loses a point. If he can't relate to the first word himself, he can cop-out with a rhyme. If he can't do either in ten seconds, he bombs out on another point. 'kay?' If this doesn't convince him that it's a fun experience add, 'Darling, I know it sounds diffie, but really it's hugely evocative.' This'll get 'em even if they don't understand it any better than you: it sounds terribly European, and you know how collectable Americans find us. In fact throw in the word 'frightfully' and you'll probably get a proposal too.

misconceptions on a general level, so I don't aim to try. On the other hand, as the ladyfriend of Jenkins, you are fag designate so I'll try to give you a little insight into your new position.

Rather A Nasty Habit

Nowadays few public schools openly admit to having a fagging system as was illustrated by an aviary of well-known Beaks in a recent Sunday Supplement article. Each claimed to believe that the habit was a nasty one, and had been abolished in his school. This proves nothing except that you can't believe all that you read in the papers, even when a schoolmaster has the bye-line.

The fact is that though only one or two public schools have a properly organised system of fagging any more, most still have an illicit one whereby when a senior boy in a bate yells 'JUMP!' twenty little chaps charge off in search of the trampolines. In older, more structured times, the command would be pre-fixed by the words 'Fag!' or 'Boy Up!' or something equally degrading. Today a politer, more democratic vocative is employed such as ''ere, you!' In other words nothing has really changed that much, which is why henceforth I shall refer to all forms of big boys bullying little boys as Fagging.

Fagging started, as I mentioned earlier, in that mournful period when rich ignorant yobs joined the poor intellectual snobs at School. The basic principle was survival of the fittest, physically rather than mentally. In other words the big thick boys beat weedy brainy boys to the other side of eternity and back and therefore proved that might may not be right, but it's unwise to say so if you're a seven stone weakling. By this method, they more or less turned education and Christian morality upside down with one fell boot, and often literally at that.

The masters in those days were absolutely in awe of the boys, partly because they were anti-thumping generally, partly because they were far too outnumbered to try thumping individually, and partly because thumping the son of the hand that feeds you is usually a bad move. So they sought to defend their ineptitude by rationalisation.

Thuggery, they said, in about four times as many words, was a good thing. It was a useful illustration of how a society governs itself and therefore was a top-hole preparation for life in the Big Bad World, though what they knew about that beats me. OK, all right, fair enough, they admitted, there were one or two casualties, but you had to look at the circumstances, the background and, quite probably, the diets of the chaps and you'd see that everything was quite understandable. And if you didn't what could you expect a poor benighted Classics master to do about it?

It seems to me that similarly archaic arguments for the basic breakdown of law and order in schools are rehashed by some of our modern, sociologically aware educationalists yet everyone thinks they are amazingly enlightened and innovative. I wouldn't like anyone to believe I didn't go along with this, I'm sure they *are* concerned and everything, but why hasn't anyone suggested that their rationalisations are no more enlightened than those of their eighteenth-century forebears in that nobody likes being hit. Probably because there's some truth in it, I suppose.

Anyhow, one way and another things got better on the fagging front. For one thing, Games were invented as a method of legalised free-for-all, and for another the masters took up Kung Fu or something. The net result was that though the system persisted, it became much less violent, and in some ways was even a bonus.

Emotion Makes Work For Homesick Boys

Even though your average 92-carat Jenkins first went away from home at the tender age of eight, he is not prepared for the onslaught of Public School on his senses. Prep School was tiny whereas this place is vast, and it seems to be so serious as well. The difference is astonishing and frightening.

Personally, I think it's quite understandable. Mamma Jenkins was allowed to choose the first school, but Papa brooked no such liberalism when it came to choosing the next.

When it was down to the Old Dear, her requirements were simple: a clean, warm, family-ish environment where a boy might learn the odd thing or two without undue discomfort. The Old Boy, bless him, has his own singular ideas, and his criteria are not infrequently bizarre, and very frequently have little to do with his son, at least as far as the untrained eye can see.

Of course, it's easy enough if the child can follow in father's footsteps (cf. above) but if he can't, there is a right to-do. Central heating has been known to throw a spanner in the works, as I've already suggested, but sometimes quirks, though more common, are less easily defined at the time. For example when the parents of my best friend's Jenkins went questin' for a school, Mrs Jenkins was much perturbed to find herself left to deal with prospective housemasters alone, her spouse unaccountably disappearing shortly after they arrived in the school grounds. Needless to state, she was agog with curiosity and speechless with anger, the latter reaction being born of a fear that the housemaster might think she was a single parent family. Somehow or another she managed to keep her counsel through sixteen school tours, knowing full well that if she voiced her queries she would only provoke Mr Jenkins into further subterfuge.

Her patience was well rewarded. On the way home from the seventeenth School Sales Pitch Mr Jenkins yawned, stretched and declared himself well content. Their persistence had paid off. Young Jenkins had a School to go to.

'Oh good, darling, I'm glad you liked it too!' said his good lady evenly. 'Tell me, what decided you, in the end?' she added, knowing it couldn't have been the impressive length of the scholarship boards in the main hall.

'The lavs, of course,' replied Mr Jenkins astonished. 'The ones there were quite good health-wise, and even the filth was quite clean.'

Mrs. Jenkins gurgled a little as she tried to decode this communication. At least she knew where he had been disappearing to now, she reflected, and wondered why she hadn't guessed before.

'Yes, some of the muck they write on the walls these days is simply dreadful. This place had the merit of lacking all allusions to perversions.'

Without clues like this to go on, it is small wonder that Jenkins finds it hard to work out why he has been sent to a particular school, and the effort of attempting to understand slowly becomes too much for him. Just before he goes under completely he is made a Fag.

This happens about three weeks after he enters the school and a wise policy it is too. You see, after three weeks it is felt that the child is familiar enough with his new conditions to conclude that he has been sent to prison. This has nothing to do with his physical surroundings, it's just that he can't actually get out. 'Course the conviction that he might possibly deserve to be punished does not help. This is not because he has a criminal mind, but because he has an overriding guilt complex – a hangover from Prep School where misdemeanours dismissed as trivia in the real world are regarded as sins worthy of the most lurid and horrid punishments. The poor child begins to wonder if he farted in chapel inadvertently, or ate off his knife? It must have been something fairly awful to end up in this educational Alcatraz.

In other words the child is thinking too much, and as a result becoming morose, introspective and homesick. As all these complaints are known to be contagious the System rolls into action and controls the situation before it gets out of hand. In short Jenkins is made to Fag to take his mind off things.

Young Warrior Brave

As you probably know, most primitive communities have their initiation rites, and Public School is no exception. Like his tribal counterparts the initiate Jenkins is set apart from the mainstream and forced into the company of his immediate contemporaries. Funnily enough the immediate effect is a positive one as a kind of enforced bonding takes place amongst the lads. This is a wonderful development as, odd though it may seem to a gregarious female soul, Public Schoolboys tend to ignore each other when they first start Public School. Goodness knows why. I can only assume that they daren't open their mouths for fear of somebody putting the boot in, but this is mere speculation.

At all events Fagging puts a stop to all this isolationism and encourages the foundation of a sort of consciousness raising group. Bands of greenhorns huddle together and murmur low, only springing apart when an older boy passes by.

From their expressions you might assume they are discussing the facts of life or something since most of them look very shifty at this stage of their development. This is not the case: bawdy badinage is a treat as yet in store. In fact the matter of the moment is really terribly dull. They are simply swopping ideas on how to beat the system. They see themselves as a little revolutionary cell, and if this is fanciful, well, at least it keeps them out of trouble.

The inspiration for subterfuge comes from their elders, for there is nothing like a common enemy for uniting people. In this case the catalyst is provided by those seniors whose useful mission it is to play fascist and thus propagate the Dunkirk spirit in their underlings. Vast plots are made for their overthrow and battles for freedom are planned to such an extent that you'd think that every one of them had been sired by J. Bond Esq., or possibly Biggles when he had the time. All this has little effect on The Powers That Be however; they've already been through this stage themselves, and it's a rare Jenkins who can teach an ex-Fag new tricks.

After all this you probably think that poor old Jenkins had a terrible time when he was a Fag. If you actually ask him about it you will be even more convinced. To be a Fag, you will be told, is to live through Armageddon before you can even pronounce it, to experience purgatory while you are still alive and spotty, to become a pessimist without knowing there was an alternative. In face by the time he has finished, you'll be so touched that your hanky will look as though it has been hit by a monsoon.

Do not be fooled, gentle reader, that's my advice to you. All this is very far from the truth. Jenkins is simply acting a part, which he does rather well. So you'd better learn now, that even when he seems to be drowning, if you throw him a line, he'll only ham it up.

Hell On Earth

If you really want to have a little malicious fun persuade Jenkins to relate what befell him in his Fagging days. Don't be put off by the drooping head, ashen cheeks and so on. Steel yourself. Have a quick shufti at a Chinese Torture Manual, go in there with the third degree and don't let up until he tells the truth. Oh, and don't feel too badly about doing this: the confession will fail to shock even the most gently born, honest!

You see things were never really as bad as he'd like you to think, or not in his day and age anyway. Tossing boys in blankets till they were sick went out of fashion ages ago, and modern duties are lenient, especially for the fleet of foot, since most schools operate on the principle of last home first abused. Which could explain why when Jenkins yells 'darling' in tones that cleave through the love-nest it perturbs him that you are the only one to answer the call. The reason being that in his mouth the endearment is roughly interpreted as 'Fag' and he is expecting ten pairs of eager little feet to pelt towards him, ready to pander to his every whim.

Even when a boy *was* the last to arrive the task set him hardly makes you think that by comparison Zeus put Atlas on community service. Witness the following example, finally related by a reluctant Jenkins who cracked when threatened with no supper.

It all began when his Fag Master wanted a scrambled egg, he said, quivering like an aspen in a tornado. A scrambled egg! I echoed, scandalised. (At these moments of true feeling it is wise to maintain a grave aspect and emote in kind, or Jenkins will feel you are underrating his ordeal.)

Not surprisingly my friend hadn't a clue how to scramble an egg at the tender age of fourteen. In fact, he's just mastering the art now, and he's twenty-nine. At that time his theory was that all you had to do was crack the egg carefully, and if you poured the contents out at the right angle a fluffy yellow mass of pure culinary joy would plop onto the toast. He put it to the test, and that was the end of one egg and one piece of bread.

After a few moments' reflection he decided that a quantum jump of the imagination was required. Fire! The revelation, I gather, was similar to that experienced by the Stone Age person who dropped one flint on top of another and ended up with a singed fringe. Forgetting to dedicate anything to the gods for their help, he set off hotfoot for the chemistry lab. This last oversight shows, I think, that Jenkins has much to learn from his ancestors.

Anyway, once in the chemistry lab, he pretended that he was J. Bond stealing Soviet secrets and managed to bag a Bunsen burner undetected. Spurred on by his success, he shimmied into the kitchens and relieved the unwitting chef of one industrial sized casserole. In next to no time he was back in his House, looking for a gas outlet.

Power found, he cracked the remaining five eggs available to him into the casserole and gave them a quick whisk with his fingers. At first he couldn't work out what the black bits were that were floating around in there, but then he remembered he hadn't showered very well after the soccer game that afternoon, and that little mystery was solved. He held the pan over the flame and waited. The first thing to be burned was his hand. Enamel casseroles, as he discovered, conduct heat alarmingly well. He soldiered on, however, flesh a-sizzle, for by now the mission was all.

He soldiered on – by now the mission was all

Some twenty minutes later, long after Tea was over and the Fag Master was in his study angrily and hungrily poring over his Pliny, poor little Jenkins appeared with his version of scrambled eggs on toast. The whole snack was served in the casserole as Jenkins couldn't ungum the charred egg from the bottom of it. As for the toast, he threw that on top, more to show willing than anything else. It struck me that he really should have had a word with the gods beforehand, but as he pointed out they got their burnt offering in the end.

'Oh, you poor lamb' I whispered sympathetically. 'What did *they* do to you?' Castration at least, I thought, judging by the look on his face. 'They made me buy six new eggs,' he said. I thought this was rather lenient considering he had burned the toast as well but I didn't say anything: the memory had been such a trauma that Jenkins needed a drink, and I went to pour it. Now was no time to preach temperance, still less to hint that I sympathised with the other side.

If this doesn't convince you that all the ballyhoo about the horrors of Fagging is no more than hot air, you are a terribly gullible girl. I shall have one last attempt at making you see sense, and then you're on your own.

After various tests, Jenkins was at last deemed ready for the final ordeal. If passed, his Fagging days would be behind him and so he waited stoically to hear what the Herculean task would be.

'Find out what size bra Josie takes,' came the command. Jenkins reeled. Never in his most lurid nightmares had he imagined that he would be forced into the room of a sixth-form female, and worse, into her underwear drawer. The mere thought of it brought him out in a cold sweat.

For a couple of days he shirked the challenge. He

became introverted and morose, and at last confided in a fellow Fag.

'Holy Mother of God!' said the other, who happened to be a Catholic.

'She might as well be,' agreed Jenkins balefully.

'Well,' said his friend after a silence which showed he appreciated the tragedy, 'It's a bad one, I grant you. But do you want to be a Fag for the rest of your life?'

That did it. With fantastic daring and consummate stealth Jenkins accomplished his mission and came up with the magic number 78B.

'Good Lord!' I said involuntarily interrupting his rhetoric. 'What *did* they say to that?'

'They laughed, most of them,' he told me bitterly. 'But what made things worse was that one of them stood up for me. I was right, he said. I should have smelt a rat then, especially when everyone went quiet. Apparently they didn't know that Josie's mum was French and bought metric bras. Jenkins Ma knew all the time. He was going out with her!'

'Oh?' I said, nonplussed.

'You just don't understand, do you?' said Jenkins. 'It was Jenkins Ma who set the test. I'd been betrayed. It was hell.'

I thought about this and decided that if Jenkins was right the devil was a dull creature indeed, which cheered me up a lot. It's an ill wind, you know.

Paradise Regained

Fortunately for young Jenkins he does not remain a Fag all his life. One fine day he turns into a senior and starts bossing people around himself. Sometimes, as shown above, his own experiences as a slave labourer can have a softening effect, but this is not always the case. And to reassure you that Jenkins's attitude to you as permanent Fag is better than his attitude to those who used to serve under him, I have a little story to relate about one Jenkins whom I knew particularly well. He calls it a minor aberration on his part, and was actually rather reluctant to tell me the tale at all. I think he feared a complete sense-of-humour-failure on my part. Judge for yourself if he was right or not.

It transpired that Jenkins and his coterie were at war with their opposite numbers in a neighbouring house. Both camps devoted all their creative energies to thinking up nastier and nastier presents to send to each other. After a swingeing blow delivered by the opposite side, gloom descended on Jenkins and chums. They could think of no way to better the insult than sticking the prefects' loo roll together with bits of chewing gum.

Suddenly my friend was hit with inspiration. Thus it was he who took the credit for the bizarre sight of a small boy of about fourteen years diligently tailing the housemaster's bull mastiff. From the light in the child's eye one would have thought that he was on the trail of a mass murderer. Not so. His somewhat less newsworthy objective was to collect some of the animal's droppings 'while they were still fresh', pop them into a shoe box, gift wrap it, and lob the whole thing into the enemy common room. He was further detailed to imply that this was a peace offering, and being a good little fag he followed the instructions to the letter.

The opposition fell upon the parcel with savage eagerness. No doubt they expected to find chocolates and wine under the pretty ribbons. Imagine then their disappointment when they discovered the truth of the matter. No wonder they threw the whole lot at the bewildered Fag, who caught it full on the shirt, and later full on the ear from Matron who had enough problems with the laundry staff as it was, without that sort of thing.

At least – I thought, when he had finished the story and sat weeping with laughter – at least no woman could be expected to carry out such a task. Such high jinx are no more than the excess of youth. For once I was right.

As fate would have it, Jenkins and I were at the same party a few weeks later. Gently weaving in and out of the small talk I chanced to spy a youngish chap looking at Jenkins with stars in his eyes. Now Jenkins is no Adonis and he isn't noted for his philosophy either so I was perturbed to see someone looking at him as though he was a guru. Intrigued, I pointed Jenkins in the direction of his only known fan. 'My Fag,' he cried, well pleased. 'Come and be introduced.'

It was a chastening experience. As we talked I learned that the boy whom I had pitied so shortly before had obviously found the meaning of life while waiting for a bull mastiff to defecate and thought Jenkins was a bit of a hero. Somewhat dazed I related his remarks to the object of his adoration. 'I can't say I'm surprised,' said Jenkins, 'it was the turd that did it. Showed him what was what. I only wish I could do the same to the girlfriend to make her appreciate me. But no, she's a woman. Doesn't see things in the same light. I shouldn't think she does anyhow, and I wouldn't care to try to find out with Camilla.' Which shows that he has learned something along the way. The reaction of the younger man prompts another observation about Fagging: once a Fag always a Fag. The pity of it is that no Fag served two masters and mistresses don't come into it.

The Cruellest Cut Of All

While I was researching this book I found that my friends helped me along by supplying funny stories and anecdotes. They did so quite spontaneously and though I'm fairly grateful for this in the main, there were times when I got a bit fed up with their enthusiasm. For instance, I was in my kitchen one evening trying to breathe some life into an expired souffle, when I heard my own Jenkins recounting an episode not unlike that of the scrambled eggs.

'I suppose you were a terribly nice Fag master yourself?' remarked my friend Elinor when he had reached the heart-rending summit of his tale.

'Naturally,' rang the reply. 'By the time I got to that stage I realised the whole system was antiquated and barbaric. The first thing I did was give my Fag a cookbook. And apart from the odd souffle all I asked was that he kept my study in order, picking up socks when necessary and so on. You know the sort of thing. Posting the odd letter, polishing the odd shoe. But I didn't let it get out of hand. Oh, no. You have to maintain some of the old standards don't you think? Yes, well, I let him call me Sir, to keep him in his place, as it were.'

'Like Rebecca, you mean? said Elinor elegantly.

In the quiet of the kitchen I thought about this and it occurred to me that I had a lot in common with a fag. It was, after all, about three weeks after love blossomed that I began my Duties. Goodness knows what he was trying to take *my* mind off – it can't have been homesickness. I did know, however, that there were no jolly side-effects like camaraderie. My only companion in the kitchen was his dog, and he was against me anyhow, since before I arrived the right hand side of the duvet doubled as a kennel. Perhaps I ought to start calling him Sir, I thought.

'Whatever's the matter?' said Elinor as she joined me in my cell.

'Fags!' I spat. 'They can ruin your love life!'

'You sound like a government health warning.'

'Maybe I should be,' I told her blackly.

'I shouldn't put that in the book,' she said, 'you'll only depress people.'

I'm not so sure. After circulating a short questionnaire, I realise I am far from alone in my doldrums and I think that you, like me, may like to know that there are others crewing the same leaky boat, if you see what I mean. There's safety in numbers, after all.

Homework

1. Find out the name of your beloved's Fag Master, object of hero-worship or whatever.
2. Cast caution to the winds and engineer a meeting.
3. Extract from him any tales of the boyish Jenkins that might embarrass him now he's grown up.
4. Type them up neatly and store them in a locked filing cabinet. This is your insurance policy/ blackmail material. Once Jenkins knows that you are in possession of the grim details of his past he will mind his Ps and Qs far more. After all, if he provokes you too far, you might embarrass him in public by telling one of these choice anecdotes, mightn't you?

   Come, come, why the shock? You're in this game to win, you know.

Playing Up

Everyone knows that England invented Team Spirit, Fair Play and Being a Good Loser. Most people also know that the battle of Waterloo was won on the playing fields of Eton, and though this confuses the Belgians no end, it does show how important the whole sporting thing is to the Brits in general and Public Schoolboys in particular. So if you're going to play with a Jenkins, you'd better understand his sporting ethics. If ethics they be.

The Inner Game

One little known fact about Jenkins and sport is that he has an on-going competition with the school itself. The older he gets, the fiercer the fight. This is basically because he would rather be running a harem instead of running the four-minute mile, but the school's preference is the other way around. I think this is because Public Schools regard sporting activities as the antidote to sexual frustration; whenever a boy gets tropical around the gills, he is sent for a seven mile gallop in the pouring rain. Apparently the thinking behind this is that the run will exhaust him so much that he will be too tired to sustain passion, or the rain will bring on an attack of pneumonia which will land him in the san for a week or two, where the sight of Matron will put paid to any untoward fantasies in double quick time.

Whether this rationalisation is right or wrong, it does give you a clue as to why sex and sport are so irrevocably intertwined in Jenkins's mind. You may have noticed how he has a way of equating the calories spent with a lady to the equivalent number of miles he would have to run to feel at peace with the world. Or maybe it stems from the fact that the only way the Physics master could bash the idea of man-foot-pounds into those fetid little minds was to throw in the odd allusion to horizontal jogging. I really couldn't say. The only reason I mention it at all is to sustain you through those awkward moments when Jenkins grins hugely and says he's just accomplished a five mile run, when you thought he'd been up to something entirely different.

The Game's The Thing

Whatever the reasons for its dominant role in the school curriculum, sport really does play an extremely important part in Jenkins's formative years. It is as though some Governor once dreamed that life was one long sprint from the cradle to the grave and wanted to be sure that all his boys knew how to pace themselves. This could explain why Jenkins is apt to spend a lot of time chasing wild geese – he needs the exercise – and why he has a distinct propensity to confuse motion with progress. You only have to pay a quick visit to the Stock Exchange, which in many ways is an extension of Public School, to see what I mean.

On the other hand, maybe the old Governor just wanted to encourage the boys to sing their own songs. It is well known that rugby players all chant together in the communal bath and that their ditties are seldom any cleaner than they are. When Jenkins puts lyrics to music, he takes smuttiness to new depths, probably because he's got such a wide vocabulary, and can even be obscene in classical tongues if necessary. I know at least one mob of boys who have taken the idea of music by the people for the people to the ultimate nadir. Not one of them can play an instrument and they're all tone deaf, but this has not deterred them from forming a band with the express purpose, apparently, of giving sexual counselling from the concert platform. Whenever they play, strong men blush and rush to cut off the electricity supply, and judging by the fact that they only sold sixty singles out of a run of 1,000 they aren't destined to appear on your television screen. I would love to give you an excerpt from one of their songs as an educational exercise, but decency and fear of the censor prevent me . . .

Aside from balladry, the wonderful thing about sport is the astonishing variety of games that Jenkins can be called upon to play: Squash, Racquets, Fives, (the two different sorts being the Eton variety and the Rugby variety and neither, with the curious numerical inaccuracy of Public School, is ever played by more than four people) and many many more. It is because of the wealth of games played by the English Public Schoolboy, I am led to believe, that Britain will ever have a place in the history of the world, for wherever we sent our boys to build an empire the grand old tradition of fair play is continued by the natives. The sad bit is that these days they beat us, of which more later.

The most important games, beyond a shadow of a doubt, are soccer and rugby. Public Schools are pretty much divided down the middle as to which one they play, and never the opposing twain shall meet nae more. There *was* a time when Eton, a soccer school, used to meet Westminster, a rugby school, for an annual match which was a kind of hotchpotch of the two. The confusion was appalling and the casualty rate monumental but the spectators had a whale of a time. Unfortunately the event is not on the calendar these days, since it is now deemed that both teams in one game should play by the same set of rules. Ours is a conservative age.

Fortunately it is possible to enjoy a similar sort of spectacle today. To do so you have to be in the study of one of the nation's better homes on a Saturday afternoon in the winter, and there must be a representative of one rugby school and one soccer school present. It is much better fun if the teams are bigger, but these things are hard to arrange ad hoc. The vital ingredient is provided by the television companies, who must be broadcasting on one channel an important soccer match, and on another a rugby international. Your part is to mention casually that it is too wet to go out this afternoon, isn't it, and why don't we all watch the TV? Soon the battle will commence. The verbal mudslinging when the conflict of interests is discovered soon turns into physical fist-flinging and the fight is far dirtier, but much more entertaining than anything going on at either real life match. Also it usually lasts so long that by the time a compromise is reached all the Box has to offer is a party political broadcast or something equally controversial, and you can all sit down to tea and crumpets exhausted but happy.

From this you should see that Jenkins is liable to be a bit of an extremist about sport, so it is important for a girl to have a working knowledge of the more common games if she wishes to avoid nasty comments. You don't have to bother with elitist things like the Eton Wall Game, I'm pretty sure that 60% of the players don't understand it, but when it comes to other sports you will discover that ignorance is far from bliss. In fact if you should be foolish enough to ask why the ref doesn't stop that Welshman from cheating since he obviously shouldn't be tearing around with the ball under his arm, you'll soon discover what the literal meaning of to be squashed feels like. Therefore I suggest you go to the library and mug up on all the major ball games mentioned above, plus cricket. If you are being taken to Henley for the final throes of the Regatta, rowing jargon is also on your study list. For it may seem reasonable to you to ask how Bow can possibly catch a crab on the upper reaches of the Thames, crabs tending to prefer the seaside and all, but I can assure you to my cost that the question is quaintness itself to Jenkins and all his coterie.

Setting A Good Example

There is a mystical side to this games lark. It is embodied in Team Spirit, which for Jenkins is nearly the same as Holy Spirit. When he is in a team he seems to transcend his lesser self so that when he scores 922 goals he hangs about the pavilion modestly saying it was team work, rather than bragging, as he does about all other achievements. Which is why he has little time for the prima donnas of the professional field.

It is hard to say from whence this modesty springs but team spirit has advantages. If you're up to your neck in muck with your friends, fighting the common foe, you don't worry about the conditions, the game must be played and your team must win. Some people have said that this could explain why the officers in the trenches in the Great War let the whole ghastly shemozzle go on so long, but I think this is a simplistic view of the matter and certainly jolly unkind and I'm sure you agree.

To be perfectly honest the whole team thing probably has its roots in history, like every other part of school life. I think that the point about the effect of the influx of the gentry on the poor scholars has now been laboured enough to bring it home to the least receptive of you. I have also noted that there is nothing like the common enemy for uniting people. What better way of leaping the class barrier than lumping all the types of boy into a team to fight another set of equally mixed people? It also proves that brain and brawn can be usefully united in that there's not much point in having a kick like Pegasus if you can't think where to aim. If you follow my gist.

I have already said a bit about the way games was one of the biggest exports when we had an empire, and now it is appropriate to tell you why. We exported to Set A Good Example. If a good pelt round the fields can stop Public Schoolboys using each other as punchbags it must be an antidote to sectarian riots in Nepal as well. All right, it was a patronising view to take, and it didn't work, but it probably seemed like a good idea at the time.

And it hasn't entirely died out either. Wherever there is mass unemployment and urban unrest, the finest thing the Powers That Be suggest is the building of a sports centre. Who said we were starting to learn from history? And more to the point, who said Public School influence on society was dying out?

Winning Doesn't Really Matter

The point about a good game is that it is played well, and that we should forget who scores the most goals; or at least this is what Jenkins thinks. This is hardly shattering news to an English girl whose veins flow with similar blood, but it certainly stymies the rest of the world. It's an idea that takes years to get used to and probably explains why we had such difficulty in converting our colonial subjects.

I mean, look at it from their point of view. They haven't inherited the Jenkins outlook on life in general and games in particular, so they act rationally. As far as they can see a game is essentially a combat situation and so they do their level best to win.

At first Jenkins lets this pass calling it beginner's luck, and 'makes allowances' for all he's worth. Despite this, his patience runs out as his protégé goes on winning, and worse, crowing about his prowess. Sooner or later the pupil notices the expression on Jenkins's face and enquires why he looks so pained.

'Look, the thing is, well, frankly, you simply haven't grasped it,' Jenkins explodes with questionable lucidity.

'Uh?' says his astonished pupil who thought that he'd grasped everything rather well and was doing capitally.

'Yes, no. Well, the thing is your attitude,' continues Jenkins.

The other gurgles, nonplussed.

'I mean you're just not playing the game, old man.'

Bewilderment of a terminal nature sets in.

'What I'm trying to say is that you don't need to be so damned aggressive. Winning doesn't really matter, you know. It's being a good loser that counts!'

Exit natives in search of shrink for Big White Fool who has now proved for all to see that going out in the mid-day sun has finally got the better of him: he's talking gibberish.

'Course all this business about being a Good Loser refers back to Jenkins's fear of commitment and adulation of amateurishness and I'm not at all sure it's a clever philosophy. It's all very well being a Good Loser when the Australians wipe the floor with our boys and hang on to the Ashes like grim death, but it's

'Winning doesn't really matter, you know'

quite another being a Good Loser when the Japanese take a perfectly good British innovation, make it smaller and wipe us off the face of the Dow Jones Index. I mean, it's not as though Britannia has a lot of spare cash these days.

I can only hope that the sports masters of the future will tell the boys that although being a Good Loser is important they don't have to feel obliged to throw in the towel in round one. There is such a thing as a Magnanimous Winner, you know.

Indoor Sport

This is about board games. I daresay we'll get around to the other indoor sport later.

Indoor games are fantastic phenomena in Jenkins's life as they seldom involve teams; therefore no team spirit is required. This means that the boy can be unspeakably nasty and cheat to his heart's content. So if you have ever accused your Jenkins of positively lying about a backgammon throw, take it from me, you were right.

It all goes back to his early days, this lack of honour. Put him in front of a chessboard, or even snakes and ladders and in his mind's ear he hears the torrential rain of a winter Sunday in the Cotswolds. It is too wet to go out so all the little boys have been cooped up all day. They are restive, fractious and ready for blood, then the housemaster gets out the games trunk.

In other words, a games board or pack of cards is a memory trigger for Jenkins. The memory it triggers is a nasty one and he acts accordingly. Quite frankly I would avoid the situation altogether if I were you.

My friend Sara tells of an unpleasant occasion when her Jenkins was routed at backgammon by his friend. He was so incensed by this that he refused to say goodnight to anyone and went to bed at ten o'clock in the slough of sulks. Apparently he felt that since the other man was a guest in his house he should have shown his appreciation of the hospitality by allowing his host to win.

The next morning things seemed to be better and they all set off for the pub. Sara was driving the car, her friend Antonia was in the passenger seat, and the opponents of the night before occupied the back. Things ran fairly smoothly for a bit, then:

'God, you're funny when you lose a game,' said the heartless guest, 'and you've always been the same, ever since we were at Prep!'

'Well,if you'd played fair, I would have won,' moaned Jenkins.

'*Me* play fair? I like that! You cheated on the second throw, you moved two double sixes and you only got fives.'

'I did not.'

'You did!'

And shortly after that all Sara could see out of her rear view mirror were flaying arms and tufts of hair. She is still trying to come to terms with the shock of seeing two men of 28 years behaving like a couple of nine year olds and has not been herself of late.

Now perhaps you see why I would recommend that there are certain forms of indoor sport that you should never, ever play with a Jenkins.

Mixed Singles

While you're setting yourself up as Jenkins's ideal partner, you will no doubt begin to see that Gamesmanship can lose its charm. You only have to listen to him sometimes and you get the feeling that you're dribbling down the right wing, and this is not always as exhilarating as it sounds. As my friend Isabella once ruefully remarked, 'When you've just been through a 28 hour labour and presented the sod with twins you'd expect him to come out with something a little more loving than 'well played', wouldn't you?' Quite.

The one that gets me is the constant cry of 'that's not cricket'. When I am in a towering rage over the state of the world, and so totally at odds with Jenkins that I have just delivered the shrewd death-thrust to his argument, I know that it's not cricket: it's a full blown row, that's what it is, and where the sound of leather on willow comes into it beats me.

'Course if I actually give voice to these feelings, Jenkins sighs a lot, and chucks a hopeful look at the ceiling as though expecting it to prove its solidarity with him by falling on my head. The tension is usually only broken when he says 'Still I can't expect you to fight fair. You're only a woman.'

This is my cue to leave the room, for nothing makes me feel more murderous than a self-satisfied Jenkins and I strongly suspect that when it comes to manslaughter, prevention is tons easier than cure.

Another hazard of entering the oldest sparring ring of all with the athletic Jenkins is that he will endlessly forget that you aren't one of the chaps. Thus you will be thumped on the back as though you had colic at the slightest provocation. You will also be expected to play by the rules (always a dodgy one with Jenkins in that when he is playing with girls he is apt to change them at the drop of a hat), give him a sporting chance and never, ever catch him on a sticky wicket even if you have one handy. And remember, if you tell him that one of his cuddles makes you feel like the ball in a rugby scrum, he will probably take it as a compliment.

On the other hand, you may end up with one of those Public Schoolboys who hated every moment that they spent braced against gales for the good of the school and if this is the case you will soon learn that this type can be equally trying. It is as though the whole process inflicted a deep psychological wound for which there is no known cure.

These are always the chaps who come off worst. They were mobile magnets who attracted every sporting disaster known to man, and it is only the cruellist twist of fate that prevented them from getting into the Guinness Book of Records as Most Injured Human In The Solar System. They broke legs playing football, cracked ribs rowing boats and were annually scalped by bouncers on the cricket field. They are fated to suffer from these scars eternally, and you, dear reader, will be doomed to sympathise all the way down the life-line.

The worst thing about the non-sporting Jenkins is his conviction that he did enough jiggering around at school to exempt him from locomotion for the duration of his mortal coil. This means that once he's taken you on, you'll have to do all the running. If your Jenkins falls into this category I'd save up for a motorised bath chair, and have done with it if I were you.

In short, the message of this chapter is that however fair-minded you are, you've got to play mean and tough if you want to get anywhere with Jenkins. If he ever complains just bat your eyelids a bit and say you were following his example. That'll shut him up.

Homework

1. Learn for yourself the contents of a sports bag.
2. Learn to recite them without retching or blushing.

The Revolting Stage

Though you may find it hard to believe, Jenkins does have a latent Che Guevara instinct. Buried deep in his conventional breast is the spirit of revolution and from time to time it rears its free thinking little head. I find this terribly exciting, because you never know when it's going to crop up. Anyway, you wouldn't want the poor chap to spend his whole life in a mental straight jacket, now would you?

You don't have to answer that.

Happy Hour

In the lower forms* a boy has few opportunities for self-expression. He might occasionally thump someone who disagrees with him or steals his tuck, by way of asserting individuality, but otherwise he is content to let his character break through only at the allowed time, that being the period between afternoon tea and prep.†

* Forms: By this I mean a year band of pupils at school. Naturally most Public Schools have their own name for this, but just for once I decided to give you a break and use the word that the rest of us understand.

† Prep: In this case 'prep' is another way of saying homework. It is short for preparation. In this context it has nothing to do with 'Prep' with a capital 'p' which is short for Preparatory, and means the educational establishment where Jenkins lodges between the ages of eight and thirteen.

This is the witching hour at Public School, when any housemaster with an ambition to reach senility with all his limbs on leaves the House altogether and so the boys can let off steam undisturbed. There follows a scene of unbridled youthful energy to which the weak-hearted should never be exposed.

For this is Jenkins allowing the genes of his bestial pre-historic antecedants come to the fore. This is Jenkins, blithe hope of the privileged classes, rampaging madly from cloakroom to classroom, sap coursing hysterically through his little blue veins. This is the boy illustrating that, in truth, 10,000 years of civilisation have been but water off a duck's back to him and all his tribe. Which should make the thought that the child is father of the man strike terror into your heart.

The effects of all this happy thrashing about can be seen on the furniture. The chairs have wonky legs, desk tops have stab-wounds and in some places footprints are visible on the ceiling. But do not think that these casualties are occasioned in sheer wanton destruction – they are really the result of the quest for knowledge. An old Jenkins of mine informs me proudly that he discovered a red-hot poker will 'quite easily go through an inch or two of wood in a jiffy'. Marvellous. History remains mum as to why he needed to ascertain this for himself or what a child of fifteen was doing with a red-hot poker in the first place, but I applaud the adventurous spirit it shows.

My sentiments are shared by one or two schools who have made a tourist attraction out of the aftermath of similar recreational activities. It's nice to know that even Messrs Gladstone and Pitt were subject to that all too human urge to carve one's name on the oak panelling, isn't it?

Few forays, however, can match those of one Jenkins of my acquaintance who hankered after a career in the SAS, I think. His father, a hoary old fellow who daily expected an action-replay of the siege of Lucknow at his own Cornish seat, had accumulated enough incendiary devices in his stables to repulse a continent of foreigners and was apt to let one or two off every now and then to make sure the damp hadn't got to them. This passion for firearms had been inherited by his heir, who regularly raided the family armoury to stock up his supplies at school. You may wonder why a boy needed a private arsenal in the peaceful precincts of an English Public School, but doubtless your boyfriend will understand instantly. Jenkins needed the ammo. to blow up the housemaster's potting shed, which was the high spot of every term.

And mighty was his success at this. The resultant scorching roots meant that the Tomato Prize at the local country show eluded the poor Beak for nigh on five summers.

It is a matter for some celebration that nothing more serious was ever damaged. I should also say, before Cornwall is entirely depopulated that Jenkins was ever a sweet-tempered boy and that the love of a good woman has, in the fullness of time, persuaded him to give up closet terrorism in favour of organising Guy Fawkes night firework displays for the village.

Only one other act of equal horror springs to mind, one perpetrated by a Jenkins, that is. This lad hailed from Yorkshire where men are men and where every baronial hall is choked with explosives, apparently. Jenkins, I gather, was a young Bart much given to violent affections for pyrotechnics – so much so that he devoted one whole summer holiday to manufacturing, single-handed, a mortar bomb. The next term, the whole house clustered round for the launch. Sadly, Jenkins had done all his sums wrong, and the thing failed miserably to project. Still, the bomb did have the wherewithal to self explode and took the entire window with it on its journey to the land where legends live. I know not whether this Jenkins continues in his bizarre pursuits, but am told that he married a kennel maid. It is to be hoped, for the sake of the Ridings, that she brought him to heel.

Zen And The Art Of Vegetarian Nihilism For Heavy Metal Fans

All good things come to an end, and innocent pleasures like blowing up buildings soon give way to deeper things. When he is about 16 Jenkins becomes reclusive and enmeshed in his own private thoughts. He wants to live life to the full, so he tries to give up sleep altogether to make sure that not a moment is wasted. This of course means that he is never more than half awake, a condition he may retain throughout life, but with less and less cause as the years pass by.

Before he can get down to serious philosophy, he has to decide what he wants to discover himself to be. Unfortunately he has already learnt that you are what you eat by the time he reaches this dilemma. To help him make a decision he runs the gamut of dietary eccentricities from vegetarianism, junk-food junkie and public anorexia (he will eat in private) depending on whether he sees himself as as mystic, a Rock Star or Jean Paul-Sartre. This gives the lie to the old adage a change is as good as a rest if you happon to be on cook patrol that day.

The other immediate effect of thinking for himself is that he becomes anti-everything on the grounds that he hasn't discovered what he is pro. This is infuriating if you are trying to hold an intelligent conversation with the boy for until he hatches from his negative shell, the answer to any question is no.

Progress will not be made until he has embarked on a breakneck canter through the philosophy section of the library and a crash in modern music. Which turns him into a Kafka-esque Heavy Metal fan who is anti-vivisection and pro the nationalisation of any company his father doesn't have shares in. The confusion this causes to Jenkins himself, his family and friends is indescribable but sooner or later he calms down and follows only one of these masters with any passion.

One subject which bothers him considerably is politics. This is partly because the school's history is a catalogue of statesmen, and partly because everyone goes through a politically aware stage: it is a phase, rather like acne, though it can last longer.

The main worry, oddly, is that Jenkins becomes suddenly aware that he is not the same as other boys, but over-privileged. This is hardly one of the weightier revelations of our time, but it stings Jenkins, who by and large hates to stand out from the crowd. For though the days when street urchins lobbed rotten eggs at rich louts have long since passed, Jenkins & Co. are still the brunt of many a nasty joke about Upper Class Twits. This causes him a great deal of pain and he tries to balance this unequal world in his mind. The usual conclusion turns out to be that the whole thing is jolly unfair and that it is an awful shame that the other chaps can't go to the same sort of school. He converts to Marxism-Leninism post-haste, though what good he thinks that is going to do beats me.

Sadly, though totally dedicated to the cause, Jenkins the Revolutionary is not destined to last much longer than a term and a bit. In fact the Che Guevara posters are usually consigned to the funeral pyre a week or so after the school hols begin. For by this time his papa will be so bored with being called a reactionary old idiot by his heir, that he threatens expulsion from the will. His mother intervenes at this point and begs him to revert to capitalism in the interests of family harmony. This tender plucking of his heart strings makes him resolve to maintain henceforth a liberal attitude only to trivial things, like sex.

Don't think that Jenkins takes this lying down, though. His spirit is not yet entirely broken, but his stock is low.

He no longer recognises that he is over-privileged but imagines himself underrated instead. He starts to seek solace in drink, but even this has its drawbacks. For alcohol at Public School is Not On. Discovery leads to punishment, and as Jenkins is not the wiliest of creatures he is all too often reprimanded. Sometimes it is hard to understand exactly what the avenging master is taking exception to: the fact that the boy has been drinking or the fact that the boy is drunk. Witness a letter sent from Beak to parent where the phrase that follows caused much consternation: 'I am sure that you will be concerned to discover, as I was, that Jenkins was found to have been drinking, and, it must be admitted, he cannot hold his liquor'.

An incident, however, springs to mind where all could see the true cause for concern. A Jenkins and his friend were languishing on the crease of a cricket pitch one fine autumnal day in the company of an empty gin bottle, when they were discovered by the headmaster. The boys were roundly scolded and the gin bottle consigned to the waste bin, and neither of them, we can safely, but sadly assume, thought any more about it. No such luck for the headmaster. Finally the frustration exploded in front to the house captain. 'It's not the gin that bothers me so much,' he spluttered 'but there weren't any tonic bottles around, there isn't even a stream on the cricket pitch. Undiluted gin, *so* barbaric.' I see his point.

Before we go any further, I would like to redress the balance a bit. It should be remembered by all those who would say that Jenkins's abandonment of his principles is spinelessness that he is not in the easiest of positions to retain them, hemmed in as he is by history and so on. I would also like to point out that some of the greatest reformers that the country has ever known have been ex-Public Schoolboys. Indeed, there was a time when Jenkins, in the form of the Earl of Shaftesbury was the Goodie, while Joe Bloggs, in the shape of the nineteenth-century industrialist, was pretty much an out and out Baddie.

It might also be worth noting that in recent years traditional insistence on quasi-fascism at school at at home has driven Jenkins, yea!, unto the very brink of open revolt. The most prominent example of this is the tide of Jenkinses who have swashbuckled their way onto the air-waves and flooded television and radio with fine and acerbic satirical comedy. Hardly a major breakthrough for civilisation you may think, but then you are the child of a cynical age, my friend. Take it from me that there are those who wish the boys had been allowed to have their own way in youth instead of being made to wait, their angst bottled up, for the time when they could popularise their subversive cause later on.

Obviously this only applies to the few. After a while the average Jenkins knuckles down and gets on with mundaner destinies. From time to time dark thoughts may crowd his mind as he tries to balance all the disparities of this life, but he tends to dull the pain with the fruit of the vine and sometimes, horror of horrors, the leaves of the marijuana plant. Every so often he may do so to excess.

Now, I would not like to have you think that

Jenkins was a congenital escapist. No, he's just human like you and me and even the sons of the privileged have to soften the sharper edges of life from time to time.

Homework

1. Discover a) the names of your Jenkins's philosophical/historical heroes
   b) the music that he most identified with in his Revolting Stage.
2. Mug up on the answer to 1(a) and learn to love the answer to 1(b).

This exercise is invaluable for toning up your empathy muscles, which will be much tested when Jenkins is in a bleak phase. Understanding must be seen to be had, you know.

The Working Class

By this time you may well have decided that a life with Jenkins is not the sort of thing you are looking for, and may at this very moment be chalking the whole thing up to experience along with wearing a brace on your teeth, and all the other unpleasant things that we're supposed to see as an enhancement of life's rich tapestry. If you still haven't seen the light and are determined to confuse Jenkins with Prince Charming, then you had better learn something about his life style when he has left school.

In other words this is really about Jenkins the working man. It's a shocking concept, I know, but these days, almost everyone, even Public Schoolboys, have to put their noses fairly near to a grindstone.

Is Working Really The Thing?

The trouble, as far as Jenkins is concerned, is that he should have to earn an honest crust at all. He finds the whole thing terribly confusing, for he believes that Mother Earth should empty her cornucopia into his larder direct, without being asked. He reasons that his great-grandfather didn't have to do anything to justify his existence beyond whipping the odd slave from time to time and peppering the countryside with illegitimate offspring to give the yokels something to talk about.

If you tell him that times have changed, and that he shouldn't fret too much, we all have to toddle off to the workhouse these days, it won't do any good. It's just not the sort of argument that works with him, mainly because it is so reasonable, I suspect. He would far rather take the unreasonable and totally unproductive stance of cursing his fate for having the sort of ancestors who squandered the family fortune before he could get his eager little pinkies on the pile or, alternatively, had the sort of ancestors who didn't make a pile for him to dig into.

Marking Time

Because the idea of work is so repellent to Jenkins he expends a certain amount of creative energy in thinking up ways to avoid the issue. The main fear is that once he has a job he will have to stop being an amateur, and start being committed instead, and you know how he feels about that sort of thing.

The most popular way of stalling is to 'continue studies' which is a pretty way of describing going to university and having a terrifically good time. Academic life at this level suits Jenkins marvellously, especially if he actually does make it to Oxbridge. The life has all the fun of school, the cameraderie and pranks and so on with none of the unpleasant aspects like stroppy Beaks and no girls to speak of.

Jenkins takes to his new environment like a phoenix to flying. Unlike his fellows who did not go away to school he does not suffer any pangs of homesickness and shyness – he just spreads his wings, and takes off.

This tends to mean that he is an enormous success with the ladies. He is suave, confident and relaxed, somehow managing to exude an aura of manliness which has the poor blue-stockingettes falling like flies.

It is only when they get to know him better that they remember that in nature, Fly Traps have some very unappealing habits.

The only slight blot on Jenkins's horizon while he is at university is that his contemporaries who have not had the same sort of education can be very cruel. They take him at his face value; and in a way you can't blame them for not liking the rather high profile he presents to the world. The drunken debacles, which always culminate in the grossest sorts of practical jokes are easily misunderstood. I mean, it is hard to believe that someone who breaks the glass of the fire button and super-glues it at the 'on' position really has any sense of responsibility. You can probably appreciate their point of view. On the other hand you have to remember that Jenkins's joking is a form of release from a hyperactive duty gland. Not that I condone his behaviour, you understand.

Another thing that confuses the untrained Jenkins observer is the way that he seems to have so much time for enoyment. Why doesn't he suffer from essay-crisisitis like the rest of them? Can he be taken seriously? Is he just there on a stipend because of his old school tie?

The answer is no, of course. In these straitened times no-one gets a stipend to university, not even mega-Jenkinses. There are closed scholarships for the house captains of various schools at some of the colleges at Oxbridge that have been unfilled for years since the only candidate simply didn't have enough between the ears to qualify. The reason that young Jenkins seems so blissfully unworried is that though school may have filled him with lots of bad habits, one of the better ones is self-discipline which means that Jenkins knows how to pace himself, and does so. There is no mystique about this. In fact it is a very basic reaction to learning from a very early age that if you don't meet the deadlines and commitments set by the familiar harpies of society, you end up being punished horribly.

Which observation leads me to the arrogant and no doubt vain hope that this section will enter the required reading list of all militant anti-Jenkinses about to go up to university. I mean, be fair, you chaps, he can't help being sent to that sort of school. He didn't exactly choose it for himself, you know . . .

For those boys who do not have the wherewithal or the inclination for further education, marking time is less easy to define. If one is heir apparent to the estate one may be sent to be a Jackeroo in the Australian outback or a lumberjack in the Canadian tundra, on the grounds that it will better equip one to run the family lands when one finally inherits. This is a sweet way of justifying a couple of years of hell-raising, but not a lot more. If you ask me, the idea that learning to ride a bucking bronco and so on in order to prepare one for a life of wheat-growing in West Sussex is rather hard to grasp.

The person who probably gets the most fun out of marking time is the Jenkins who has no particular talents and no inheritance to speak of. He can mess around happily for years as long as he is self-supporting, and no-one minds a bit. For instance I know one such who has spent the last ten years being a pisteur in French skiing resorts all winter, and crewing yachts around the Med. all summer. His fond mamma proudly tells her guests that her third son is brushing up on his French in readiness for the career he intends to have as a translator for The European Parliament. The fact that Jenkins's way of communicating with his Gallic comrades is as it ever was, i.e. to shout pidgin English at them slowly and deliberately, doesn't seem to worry her a bit.

Playing Shop

Sooner or later even the most reluctant among us have to settle down to Real Life and get a job. For Jenkins this is not terribly easy to come to terms with. Ever since his days at the top of the school he has had an overseeing sort of mentality. He doesn't mind supervising other people to make sure the work gets done, it's doing the work himself that he can't handle. This makes conventional career structures abhorrent: starting at the bottom of the ladder sounds altogether too much like hard work to him.

Thus he does all he can to avoid being an underling. After several job interviews during which he fails to sell himself as an instant high powered executive, Jenkins meets a few friends in the same situation for a drink. They stare into their glasses darkly for a while, wondering why no-one has spotted their obvious talents. As the evening wears on they realise that the obvious course is to form their own company and thereby go straight to the top. And so the next day the chums set off happily to get incorporated.

The organisation they set up is instantly recognisable by the plethora of Chiefs and utter lack of Indians. Which is just as well really. Any minion they might employ would be so confused by the cross-fire of contradictory commands that he would lay himself down and head for the great teepee in the sky after the first 126-hour-working-week.

In other words Jenkins, Jenkins & Jenkins PLC is characterised by chaotic inefficiency and sooner or later it folds. Ever afterwards its directors mourn its fate and talk of its lost potential with dewy eyes.

It's funny, isn't it, how the best things in angling and Jenkins's career are so often the ones that got away?

Almost The Family Firm

After the demise of his own company, if it is ever born in the first place, young Jenkins is left once again with the knotty problem of getting a real job. For those without a clear vocation, the choice is pretty limited.

The most appealing pursuits are those which most closely resemble school in one way or another: the sort of professions which might indeed have separate firms, but where in fact the competition is no more vicious than the inter-house cricket cup. Which is why few chaps from Cleethorpes Comprehensive are found to be under-writers at Lloyds. You don't hear many quaint accents at the Stock Exchange either, unless you count old Harrovian as a bizzare dialect in its own right.

The great advantage of going to work at one of these bastions of English commercial society is that Jenkins feels at home there. He has a unform to wear (pinstripes, tie etc.) and can rest easy in the knowledge that he won't stand out from the crowd even if he does have a drink or two at lunch time. Also, he will be able to slip away to the country at four o'clock on Friday afternoon without incurring any nasty whiplash on Monday morning: anyone in a position to worry about his time keeping will have left at half-past three.

This does not mean that Jenkins does not work quite hard in the few hours that he is in the office: he has to pull his weight or he will be out on his ear faster than you can say redundant. So far the unions have found no toe-hold in the hallowed halls, and since they are not likely to do so much before the second coming, Jenkins is obliged to fight the battle for survival alone, and jolly distasteful he finds it.

'Characterised by chaotic inefficiency'

The Vocations

There are a few Jenkinses who have vocations, or more sordidly, ambitions. They are to be approached with caution, for these are the men who genuinely believe the school doctrine that they were born to lead, and that they know better than everyone else what is good for us.

Nothing will stop these boys. They believe that they should have power to save us from our lesser selves and tend to be heavy in the double-cross department to achieve their end. There's no knowing where they will crop up, but their main distinguishing feature is overt charm, something a trustworthy member of the species tends to despise.

So the next time a professional Jenkins butters you up, remember: too much grease is bad for you.

The Odd One Or Two

The irresistible working Jenkins is the potty one. You can spot him a mile off. For a start he is the only one with polished heels and a dangling shirt flap while everyone is sporting clogs and a sweatshirt, or equally trendy things which Jenkins is about as likely to wear as leiderhosen or djalabe. This is the Jenkins who, much against his papa's better judgement, has launched himself on a career in the arts or media.

His unsuitability for the job, at least as far as appearance goes, is manifested in a variety of quaint ways. He is the only musician in the orchestra with his bow tie awry. Everyone else is perfect in their machine tied efforts, but Jenkins wouldn't be seen dead in anything other than the grubby strands he has knotted with his own two left fists. He is the only actor in a Noel Coward cast who tries to affect a cockney accent, hell bent on being One Of The Boys as usual, despite the fact that the boys in question are swotting up on Public Schoolese. It must be considered a blessing that Jenkins doesn't realise that he is sticking out from the crowd like a sore thumb, for, bless him, if he has taken the plunge into this ungentlemanly world it is always his own decision, possibly the first that he has really made for himself in his whole life, and he is deliriously happy.

Not that the life he has chosen for himself is entirely without its problems. In fact there are times when the situation he finds himself in gets out of control and he could easily be convinced that Atlas is playing two-ball with the earth and moon. His biorhythms have turned into discords and his mind is constantly threatening to come out in sympathy.

The reason? Well, it's obvious, isn't it?

As far as Jenkins's jaundiced eye can discern the arts are stuffed to bursting with women. Women putting their cellos where they shouldn't put anything in public. Women flinging themselves around proscenium arches often clad in nothing more than the suit they were born in. Women, in short doing all manner of things that according to Jenkins'lore they shouldn't and all in the name of professionalism.

Quite the worst, however, are the women in power. They Who Must Be Obeyed, who say 'bugger' with the best of them, then yell 'darling' at the tops of their shrill little voices causing Jenkins to live from one blush to the next.

A friend of mine hurtled into the flat one evening in a regular dither, eyes revolving like bagatelle balls, sweat oozing from his furrowed forehead. Pouring him a strengthening draught of whisky I asked what ailed him.

'Oh, don't ask me, I can't tell you!' he said, gulping. I waited in silence, knowing that he would unburden himself sooner or later. Half-way through his second glass of whisky he gave me the following blow by blow account of the past eight hours or so.

'It all started when I got in late, it wasn't my fault, you understand, but I admit I was late. I was late, just for the record, because I'd been out to dinner the night before for work's sake, not my own, and I was feeling a bit queasy when I got up so I drank a carton of orange juice. Anyway I was sitting there on the number 49 when I began to feel really ill. Well, I was standing up and there were two old ladies on either side of me and so I thought I'd better make a bolt for it. Fortunately we were in a traffic jam so I didn't get hurt, though I did only just make it in time for the technicolour yawn . . .'

'Oh, well done!'

'But then I had to wait for another twenty minutes for another bus. You know what the 49 is like. Mythical. Anyway, I got into the office eventually and got bawled out by Francesca, the producer. I tried to tell her that it wasn't my fault if I was ill and she told me to fuck off and do some work, and I am just not used to her using that sort of language. So I went back to my bit of the factory farm – which is what an open-plan office in a TV company is like in case you hadn't noticed and tried to settle down to some work. Next thing you know one of the researchers is on the line to say her coil had fallen half-way out and she was going to be late and would I tell everybody. That's not the sort of thing I want to tell anybody. I didn't even know what it was but don't bother to educate me, I do now – one of the other girls immediately went into a detailed description of the whole thing and it made my stomach turn again.'

'Nothing to what it did to hers, I should think.'

'Oh, Christ, no wonder they say a woman's place is in the home,' spat Jenkins before resuming the narrative. 'No sooner had I settled down to work than three-quarters of the office shimmied off to lunch, so I thought I'd go and make my peace with Francesca. I knocked on the door and she yelled come in and in I went and she didn't have her skirt on!'

'In with a chance, Jenkins?'

'Not likely,' he retorted passing an already sopping shirt sleeve over the fevered brow. 'She was meeting someone special for lunch. Anyway I said my bit and do you know what she did? She kissed me. Only on the cheek. But still, she didn't have her skirt on.'

'Well, I shouldn't worry, dear. She obviously didn't mind.'

'That's not the point. I saw her legs,' he said gloomily and returned to a torrid, thoughtful melancholy which is where he remained for the rest of the evening.

There is little cause for wonder that Jenkins should take all these wanton goings on rather hard, when he has been brought up to think that women are modest, demure and useful only about the house. How can he possibly be expected to cope with a tribe of Amazons who treat him with about as much respect as his nanny and almost as much affection as his big sis. He is chastised, tickled and teased and the more this brings him out in Public School spots the less clemency he is likely to receive. He squirms, flinches and eventually learns to laugh at himself. At which point the sun comes out and the monstrous regiment of women officially declare spring, and amnesty for Jenkins.

For there is no-one sweeter to the commanding female eye than Jenkins when he ceases to take himself as seriously as he takes his bowels. It might be the combination of old world charm and hopelessly old jokes that do it, or just the generally sideways view the boy has of life, as though he yet lived in an England which was still dotted with men on white chargers, golfers in plus fours and everyone of them knee-deep in cucumber sandwiches. One Jenkins I know, for example, is very useful when one is ordered to venture forth into the nether counties: he doesn't know much about the places themselves, but he can direct you to a first class bun shop in every major city in the land, and most of the market towns as well. He is also pretty good on ice-cream parlours in Tuscany.

Most Jenkinses have hidden talents of this nature, and also a rather charming way of telling stories against themselves, witness the one above. And once Jenkins sees the funny side of himself, he sees the funny side of everything else as well, and can make you laugh so much that you get side ache. Which, perilously, can be one step off heartache and wanting him to get down to business far more serious than work.

Which is why you'd better be very careful when you find yourself working with a member of the class of '65, or whatever your preferred vintage of Jenkins. You could find yourself out for a working dinner, and not long after that end up permanently out to lunch, if you see what I mean.

The Worrying Exception

You may find that Jenkins is one of those crusading types who wants to restore his family to its former glory, and a sad case he is too. He devotes himself to his cause with a zest which is almost alarming, as though driven by some particular malady which deprives him of sleep and general joie de vivre. The symptoms which make him immediately identifiable are his pupils which have dilated out of their natural neat round orbs into pound signs. Personally, I find this Jenkins a bit of a worry because, and you really must try to understand this, odd though it sounds, it is not greed which drives him but a horribly misguided sense of honour. It is a thing which many psychiatrists have managed to overlook, but is nonetheless generally accepted that a money grubbing Jenkins is not a happy one, and probably comes from a broken home or something, so you must be terrifically nice to the poor boy and keep lots of mental sticking plaster about your person.

Consolation Prize

Whatever method your Jenkins adopts to keep the wolf from the portcullis, you will be expected to be his helpmate and inspiration and there is no way that this could be described as an enjoyable activity.

On the other hand if you actually get to the stage where you are swopping vows, you can rest assured about one thing. Jenkins will move heaven and earth to keep you in the manner to which he thinks you ought to be accustomed. It would be far too embarrassing for him if he didn't.

PART TWO

The Nitty Gritty

Sooner or later everything gets back to basics. Depressing, I know, but true all the same. You know how it is: you start off with high minded, even celestial principles, but in the end you fall over those same principles and land up back on earth with a bruised backside.

So it is with this book. Originally I thought a quick but detailed exposé of Jenkins's character and background would be enough to equip any girl for the lifelong struggle falling in love with him is bound to entail.

On due reflection I realise I was wrong. Well, actually I was battered into submission by the army of faceless ladies who have contributed their quid's worth of advice to these pages. They told me it was unfair to write a text book when what you really needed was Operating Instructions, as it were. Since all these females are bigger than me I have decided to capitulate.

So fasten your seat belts. We are about to hit the brass tacks, and hard.

Warning

From here on in this tome will become increasingly indecorous. It's about interpersonal relationships (sex) and you know what that means – downhill all the way. Don't say you weren't warned.

Sex One: Overture and Beginners

Backs To The Wall Boys

There is a persistent and ugly rumour abroad and at home that all English Public Schools are hot beds of homosexuality, vice and perversion. This is not the case. Or not nearly so much the case as it is made out to be. Obviously there are one or two homosexuals in Public Schools, but then there are one or two homosexuals around almost everywhere these days and perfectly delightful people they are too. So why all the fuss hasn't died down by now, goodness only knows, but anyhow it's certainly time that it did. However, since it hasn't, and since the fuss rather than the reality bothers Jenkins greatly, I suppose we'd better have a quick discussion about it here and get the whole thing over with.

Big Boys Can Be Fruity

In an earlier chapter I mentioned that Jenkins keeps himself to himself when he first goes up to Public School. He has some mysterious and obscure reasons of his own for doing this, and an extra one is provided by the family. They warn him about the ghastliest pitfall of all in mysterious and roundabout ways, misguidedly trying to protect him from the evil which so obviously impends. Before he leaves home for his first term he will be party to a scene that goes something like this:

'Just watch out for the Big Boys, dear' his mother says mildly, not wanting to alarm him too much.

'Especially if they offer to help you with your work,' adds his sister, though how she knows is anybody's guess.

'Or invite you into their studies,' continues his elder cousin, who can be assumed to know what he's talking about since he's been through it, and speaks *sotto voce*, as if to emphasise that his is the voice of cruel experience.

'Bloody right, we don't want any ruddy fags in this house do we?' bellows his father in conclusion.

All this, as you can imagine, puts terror into the soul of the child. The worst thing is that no-one has told him what the Big Boys might do, and since he has a fairly rampant imagination, he imbues them with all the characteristics of the Marquis de Sade and Bluebeard rolled into one. When he becomes an Official Fag he gets even more frightened, on the grounds that he'll never be able to darken his father's doorstep again, at which point misery really does set in.

His contemporaries at school have all had the same sort of lecture and are equally confused. The only hope for them is that one member of the form has an older brother who can at least explain the exact nature of the beast they all fear. In the end he realises that homosexuality is no threat to him and that his elders and betters regard him as an ant to be stamped on, and thus are to be avoided but not feared. Thus reassured, he manages to put the problem almost to the back of his mind.

Noli Me Tangere

Though he more-or-less stops panicking about threats to his person, Jenkins never stops worrying about threats to his reputation. Thus he is never particularly happy on the subject of man's love for man. He will never touch another boy if he can possibly avoid it in case some nasty little oik yells 'pooftah' at the top of his voice.

A side effect of this in later life is that he is very wary of being touched by anyone at all, and covers his own morbid fears by discouraging PDAs. A PDA is a Public Display of Affection, and it is always thus abbreviated as though the very words themselves were sinful. His reason for doing so, he says, is that they set a bad example. It does no good to explain that you don't think the bus conductor will mind, since England is now a bona fide free society and even the lower classes are pretty unimpressionable these days: Jenkins can be stubborn and puritanical at times and this is one of them.

Which means if you are a naturally demonstrative and affectionate sort of girl, you're just going to have to mend your ways, if you want to keep Jenkins at all happy.

The Light At The End Of The Tunnel

Quite honestly, you shouldn't concern yourself too much with all the controversy about homosexuality. As a girl, you are quite unlikely to be courted by this sort of Jenkins, since, I'm happy to say, gay people are now no longer as oppressed as they were, and no longer feel the need, by and large, to be seen taking out young ladies for the sake of appearances.

In other words, that sort of chap doesn't like girls, and unless you have some hairbrained and totally stupid notion about saving them from their fate, you will not meet them on any other but the friendliest of levels.

Sex Two: Moving Duets

Too Much Talk And Not Enough Action

So far I have only considered what Jenkins will expect of you and what you can't expect of him, and by this stage you may be wondering what is in it for you, as it must seem as if he is a dead loss as far as women are concerned. In other words, as a normal healthy English girl you will want to know Jenkins's attitude to heterosexuality. After all, when you've spent hours mugging through the agony columns to prepare to deal with any sexual problem with your sleeves rolled up, you would like to feel that all this work is not in vain. So let me put your mind at rest. Jenkins has heard of it – sex that is.

Literally Speaking

When he is about sixteen or so, aspects of interpersonal human relationships are Jenkins's staple conversational diet, and frequently remain so. For example, when the chatter begins to flag Jenkins will simply say 'goolies' and his friends will all drown mirthfully in their beer. The peculiarly staccato sense of humour is a way of illustrating that Jenkins is a member of an extremely elitist society, mainly because no-one else sees the joke. In fact when he gets going in a pub, old ladies back off into the darts board, milk stouts a-quivering, for fear of where his innuendos may lead.

He can keep the act up for hours with an endless stream of one liners too. 'Knobs, knockers and ding-dongs' is a phrase which produces such hilarity that one becomes quickly convinced that the discussion is not centred on door furniture, and 'Bristol' has more to offer than its inhabitants would have you believe if Jenkins and Co. are anything to judge by. After half an hour or so of this knock-about comedy, when everyone has side-ache from laughing so much, 'bottoms' is the word that they fling at each other as the surefire clincher. After that they all down their ale and go home happy.

Of course, some would contend that music hall comedians win similar laughs by using similar words, but actually, this isn't so. The seaside brigade take much longer to get to the point and are far less blunt generally. Jenkins dispenses with all the preamble and goes straight for the punchline which in this case is invariably below the belt. He could never be accused of being coy, could our Jenkins.

The awful thing about all this is that if you spend long enough with a Jenkins you will begin to see the funny side of certain words too, which can pose the most embarrassing problems. I am mortified to relate that I have not been unaffected by this myself. For instance, I was introduced to a perfectly charming Articled Clerk the other day whose name was Mr Jones. If only he had been content to let the relationship remain on a formal footing, all would have been well. But oh, no, 'Willie, please,' he said with a pained expression when I addressed him by his full title. After which I simply couldn't look him in the face.

The Birds And The Bees

If Jenkins has the vocabulary to talk his way through a horizontal marathon and is theroetically the hottest thing to happen to a mattress since the electric blanket, in practice things aren't nearly so tropical. Or not at an early age anyhow.

The root of the problem, needless to state, is school. It really all began the day that the young buck was told the facts of life as related to birds, bees and sundry other fauna. Schoolmasters as a race seem to be singularly inept at this particular part of their duties, possibly because they are so inexperienced that they are only guessing anyway, or so their graceless pupils will try to tell you. Whatever the reason, the fair sex does not feature too highly in the little lectures that they give the boys. Instead they shilly shally around the matter in hand in the shiftiest fashion which can have unfortunate consequences and lead their charges to form the most bizarre conclusions.

For example, after one of these little chats a waggish young Jenkins was heard to remark that he had just been to a 'very interesting talk about the birds and the bees and I must say I am astonished how complicated it is to make honey. Yes, I think I might very well take up bee-keeping' or at least his friends thought he was being waggish until he started saving up for his first hive.

One headmaster of note decided that the whole subject was too embarrassing to talk about at all, and he told his junior masters that if he couldn't talk about what he termed 'that whole sordid damned mish-mash' he didn't see why they should be forced to do his dirty work for him. Instead he decided that they should produce a handbook for the boys, a sort of step by step manual through the act of procreation. He undertook to write the copy himself and being a bluff, old army type, he didn't mince his words. 'As you may have noticed,' began the opening sentence, 'you have something between your legs.' We live in hope, we live in hope.

The fact of the matter is that Jenkins, poor wee love, is all too well aware that he has something between his legs, thank you very much. It is something that he would rather not be reminded of too often, particularly when he is fourteen or fifteen. At this stage of his life the horrid thing causes the text book on his lap to rise and fall with all the nauseating unpredictability of a big dipper at a fair ground. To add insult to injury there seems to be no rhyme or reason to justify its cavortings. Worse still it matters not one jot that all the other boys have to go through exactly the same ordeal; for if on the other hand other fellows spot that Jenkins is riding the crest of yet another of these sickening waves he nudges his mates and they all fall about tittering gaily together. Small wonder then that the poor lamb tends to spend all the time with his legs crossed, or to put it more accurately, clamped together. And who can fault him if he looks pained? Trying to walk in a sitting position is probably agony itself.

Consequently the first few years of public school are a psychological as well as a physiological trauma for Jenkins. He has to keep his legs crossed, his back to the wall and his nose clean which is a big task to set a small boy. One can only sympathise with him when he wishes fervently to his sweat-stained pillow that there was some way he could fail to notice that there was something between his legs.

I need hardly tell you that as far as reproductive information is concerned Jenkins doesn't get very much help from his family either. The duty of explaining it all falls to his father and this is hardly a satisfactory state of affairs. The problem concerns Mr Jenkins greatly mainly because he knows that he was not backward in coming forward in his youth, and this is precisely what is worrying him about his son. He feels he ought to say something, but is hit by Jenkins Disease – acute embarrassment – and cannot think of a way to put his case. In the end he blurts something about 'most girls being somebody else's sister, probably,' and changes the subject feeling much relieved himself, though his son is vastly perplexed by the truism.

All in all, with such limited information being handed down through the ages, it is a wonder that the Jenkins tribe have managed to procreate at all.

The Creature From Outer Space

As time goes by, the unworked lurching of the text book is brought under control and the brow of Jenkins Min slowly unpuckers itself, and after the first throes of puberty school life settles down to a steady if boring pace. This happy state of affairs lasts exactly as long as Jenkins's friends and contemporaries continue to believe that girls were invented for the sole purpose of having their hair, and or legs, pulled.

This calm is but the calm before the storm. One fateful day some renegade wanders into the common room after the holidays and instead of announcing that he has a new air gun, as in the days of yore, he cleaves the air with the dramatic statement that he has got a woman. The effect, I gather, is something as cataclysmic as the first bomb on Hiroshima. For Jenkins the world will never be the same again.

Panic breaks out, as it always does when something awful happens. What is this thing a woman? comes the silent scream. No one has ever mentioned women before, or not seriously at any rate. The opposite of birds, is bees, as everyone knows. If humans do anything similar, that is really Mum and Dad's department, and Mum, bless her, doesn't seem to have been very seriously involved anyhow. Of course he knows that women are different, they have lumps on their chest for starters, and funny bits of clothing to put them in, but it has never been anything much to get excited about. Now follows a General Synod of the Unenlightened, which doesn't produce many answers. It certainly doesn't come up with a way to explain why this mate of theirs is standing there looking flushed as he yatters on about some Martian called Caroline.

Once again young Jenkins feels perplexed and unhappy. He feels he ought to get some experience, but how? He has a sneaking suspicion that this is where the blessed thing between his legs could prove useful instead of being a cross between a millstone and a yo-yo. He starts hanging around with the older boys and going to the pub for an illicit pint, where he is swiftly acquainted with the funnier side of door furniture. But where does the knob meet the knocker, and why? He says to the other boys that it's about time he got a bit of the action too, but quite frankly the only actions he knows anything about are the civil and criminal kinds, and even then the knowledge is patchy.

The Scientific Solution

Having acknowledged that he ought to find out a little more about girls, Jenkins applies himself to the task with vim. Being a wary fellow, he decides a spot of research is necessary and looks round for a suitable place to start.

His decision is apparent to his sister the moment he walks through the door at the end of this apocalyptic term. Instead of the usual grunt he beams a million dollar smile and cranes down from his great height to kiss her on the top of the head. At which point the poor girl advances to a remote state of shock: he hasn't shown this much affection since the day she taught him 'The Grand Old Duke of York' more than a decade ago. It takes a great deal of restraint to refrain from asking what ails him.

The pattern is now set for an exercise in sweetness which is apt to give even the most tolerant of girls an attack of toothache. Instead of pushing her aside to prove how macho he is, he now winds her while trying to hold the door open before she gets there. He also insists on carrying the shopping, or at least until he meets a school friend at which point he will drop the whole lot on her foot and bolt for cover. Another charming side of the new leaf is the way that he borrows her money to pay for their bus fares, usually extracting a 10% booking fee in the process. At the local burger bar he will take charge of ordering the meal, and thereby deprive the poor female of the solace of sustaining victuals since he is more than likely to order the one thing on the menu to which she has an allergy. In short he treats her as a cross between a piece of china and a wheel-chair case and it isn't much fun.

The worst thing is the conversation. At this point in his life a tête-à-tête with young Jenkins lacks a little common or garden sparkle. Once again the school is to blame: apparently he has been taught that girls only talk about clothes, cookery, soppy poetry and men. Embarrassment precludes informed discussion on the last of these so he confines his utterances to the first three. It is hard to decide who enjoys the conversation least.

As you can imagine, a great deal of fortitude is required of a girl to cope with this sort of behaviour without resorting to violence. But somehow any Sis worth the name will bide her soul in patience 'for the greater good of womankind', as she tells herself mournfully. She realises that her little brother is practising to be a Knight of the Round Table (or something equally quaint and out-moded) and knows that it is easier for him to use her as a stand-in Guinevere than to put poor old Mum through her paces.

Le Grand Debut

With any luck at all the agony won't last too long anyhow, but be terminated by the arrival of the postman bearing an embossed invitation for Jenkins. Sometimes this is not quite so dependant on chance as it seems, for there have been times when a group of sisters who all have brothers of similar ages band together and organise the event, mainly because they are sick to death of being watched as though they were escaped specimens from the biology lab, and want the boys to get on and get to grips with the real thing. Or something like it, anyhow.

Invitation received, Jenkins becomes paralysed with fright. What shall he wear, what shall he do, what shall he say? Each member of the family is called upon to give an opinion, in each case chosen for their unsuitability for the task. Papa will suggest that he wears a cravat, or something equally repulsive; Mamma will tell him not to talk about sex, politics and religion which virtually reduces him to swotting up the weather forecast, and Sis, who by this time has had enough of his problems and wants to concentrate on her own, says she couldn't care less what he does as long as he doesn't sit on anything he will regret.

This is an oblique reference to one of the horror stories encased in the Public Schoolboys Canon of Ways to Scare Younger Boys. It concerns a Jenkins who arrived at his first 'grown up' party well in advance of the appointed hour. The lady of the house, flustered and unready, ushered him into the drawing room, waved airily at the sofa, told him to make himself at home, and wafted off in search of her evening dress. Jenkins was very nervous (a state no doubt exacerbated by the sight of an unrelated woman in a bathrobe), spotted the drinks tray and decided to help himself. He had just finished pouring a gin when he heard footsteps approaching. Consumed with fright he leapt over the arm of the sofa and sat full square as though under orders to maintain his position from the highest authority in the land. Only when he stood to greet his now fully clad hostess did he realise why the seat was warm: he had been sitting on what had been until his arrival a dearly loved family pet and was now a recently departed chihuahua.

Hardly spurred on by his family and their tales of woe, it becomes Jenkins's dearest wish that the Bomb will drop the day before the party. But the fateful day dawns, noon passes and before he has time to organise a sore throat or an unstrung hamstring dread eventide is upon him. He knows it is too late to back out now, and with a heavy sense of one going to his doom, he sets off.

Once he arrives at the party he has little time to reflect on his problems, as the moment he walks through the door, he is enveloped by a mass of mates who steer him to the area they have staked out as their own. He notices that there are other clumps of settlers near-by, intrepid chaps all, keeping the faith together. Far off, in fact as far off as possible, stand a seething mass of girls who are making a revolting spectacle of themselves by giggling. Fortunately there is a gulf between them rather like that forged by Moses when he took the Red Sea to task, and for the time being Jenkins hopes it will stay as wide as it can be.

It occurs to him that the best way to cope with the

A recently departed chihuahua

situation is to get drunk. All his finer instincts tell him that this is the correct course of action, and if it isn't then why is there so much booze around in the first place? Of course, you can't really blame him. As usual school has failed to help him when he needed educating most and as he has no other data to rely on he is forced to take his model from Hollywood where, naturally, all men are superstuds. Unfortunately he hasn't yet discovered that movie moguls seldom distinguish between fantasy and reality and labour under the illusion that any fellow worth the candle can drink a dozen bottles of Tequila and still satisfy a whole convent single handed. This misconception usually means that experience is about to deal him a bitter blow.

Though the example set by Hollywood may be a reason for Jenkins's drinking it is not the only one. I happen to think that there is a deeper psychological cause. As he looks at that distant bunch of giggling English damsels the words of his father ring in his ears. These girls are someone else's sister. A friend's sister, maybe, and therefore practically his own. They all seem to dress the same way as his own at any rate. This sets him off on a series of complicated moral arguments with himself about incest, and he drinks to numb the ethical pain this entirely spurious worry causes.

For a while nothing much happens at the party and people feel a little dull. Then someone remembers it's Jenkins's debut, and all the young men gang up on him until he is forced to take action. Finally, full of Dutch courage and egged on by his friend, Jenkins, alias Macho Gringo of California lurches across no-man's land to invite one of the girls to dance. His head being in the condition it is this is hardly a wise move, as a few agonised gyrations of his body quickly prove. He reasons that all this pounding about is no more than preamble, so he moves a little closer to his partner, thinking that she too will be more than eager to get down to the nitty gritty. Unfortunately this is where the Macho Gringo bit falls apart. Those close-up shots on the silver screen just weren't close enough to give him any great insight into technique.

Which is why many a gently brought up female has rather unpleasant memories of her First Real Kiss. Blissfully thinking that Jenkins is really just an embryonic Daddy all she has in mind is a quick brush of the lips. She is totally unprepared for the sudden close encounter with Jenkins's tongue and wonders if she is supposed to swallow it or something, and worse, if she does, will she get pregnant? Usually she just chokes, and I dare say the blame for this can be equally apportioned to both sides, though I confess my sympathies lie with the young lady, especially as halfway through this dangerous encounter the booze finally overwhelms Jenkins who capsizes on top of her like a pooped parachute. I think this is the main reason why an awful lot of girls are totally misinformed about the meaning of heavy petting for so long – Jenkins is no bantam-weight to crawl away from.

Shortly after this Jenkins is ushered home by his friends. In the morning he has a megalithic hangover and no memory. Sheepishly he believes his pals, who tell him that if he's suffering from amnesia he *must* have enjoyed himself.

Lochnivar And The Tongue Sarnies

By the time the next party comes around, the lad is a little more relaxed. He knows the ropes now and considers himself to be something of an old timer when it comes to picking up girls. He has also sorted his priorities out and has an objective in view, which always makes Jenkins more comfortable. A typical conversation on this occasion will run as follows:

Jenkins: (clearing throat) Dance?
Prey: (tittering) 'Kay.
Jenkins (breathlessly and loudly because of the music) Name?
Prey: (after brief skirmish due to insupportability of his full weight on her left big toe) Henrietta.
Jenkins: What?
Prey: Henrietta.
Jenkins: No, stupid – gosh, sorry, I meant Henrietta what?
Prey: Jenkinson.
Jenkins: Henrietta Jenkinson. What a lovely name. What a lovely girl. Will you write to me when I'm back at school, Henrietta Jenkinson?

If the answer is negative Jenkins will stomp off in disgust. If it is positive, however he will revert to a refined version of the old routine and proceed with no visible decorum to the rhododendron patch and what could laughingly be described as a French kiss but what is more usually termed as a Tongue Sarnie, or even more pleasantly, a Squelsher. By the way, if you do think you might possibly end up in the shrubbery, for heavens sake, don't wear a front loading bra. As I have mentioned ad nauseam, Jenkins is a traditionalist and such new fangled ideas do not appeal to him. He gets very angry when he can't find a clasp to grapple with.

Now, the point of all this fumbling about and getting a girl to write to you is actually the pursuit of greatness. Chaps who get letters from girls are thought to be quite something at school. All the secrecy involved, the clutching of envelope to bosom to conceal the postmark, the thundering off to the seclusion of the shady oak grove to read at leisure – it all makes Jenkins Min into Lochinvar Ma. Despite what they may say, his cronies all suffer terrible pangs of jealousy as they believe Jenkins successful in love.

Which is very far from the truth, of course. Good Old Jenkins is just striking another attitude. He may seek solitude to add to the act, but once propped up against the accommodating tree, he pulls a copy of Playboy out of his pocket instead of the letter. He finds this a good deal more inspiring to read than Henrietta's despatches about hockey matches lost and the trouble she's having with Medieval History. He certainly can't be bothered with her poetry. In fact the only bit of the letter that he reads is the end, where she declares undying love and swears eternal devotion until the holidays.

Obviously this means that his replies bear little relation to the burning issues discussed by his sweetheart, but it doesn't really matter. She isn't too interested in his cricket scores or the war of attrition he is fighting with the Physics master. As for his poetry, she never gives it a second look, especially if it is in blank verse. In fact, the only bit she is keen on is, as you may have guessed, the end where he says he doesn't want to commit himself but he's the nearest he has ever been to being in love and waffles on about what they're going to do to each other in the holidays. Which at least proves that they have something to look forward to, despite the fact that their affection for each other is based entirely on fantasy and that they are barely acquainted.

Love's Young Dream

The holidays are obviously a great testing time and the expectations of the young lovers run high and wild. Jenkins Min's are colossal, actually: after weekly trips to all the chemists within a five mile radius of the school he has accumulated enough rubberwear to bring the national birth rate to a standstill.

Nine times out of ten all comes to nought. They arrange to meet under the clock at Waterloo, or somewhere equally prosaic, fail to recognise each other altogether and go their ways muttering darkly. Just occasionally things do work out, and for a while things go swimmingly. Until they find themselves alone together that is, when things begin to take a sickeningly familiar turn.

My friend Charlotte recalls one such occasion with anguish. It was a lovely day in May, she tells me, the sun was shining, a gentle breeze was blowing, God was in his heaven and Charlotte had a very pretty pink frock on. They walked in the park in the afternoon, had tea at the Ritz, for she had picked a very pretentious young Jenkins, and got on famously. In the evening they went to a rock concert which gave her a headache and then went for a meal which gave her tummy ache. By the time they reached his house she was in no mood for romance, really.

Picture the scene: low lights, low sofa, and no-one to disturb them save the dog and he's got flu, or something. The rest of the family are in France. Charlotte sitting pretty in her new pink frock and shades (to hide the stye on her eye) and Jenkins in love.

The man advances, arm outstretched, pulls off the specs, bruising her nose en passant, and whispers gently as a fog-horn 'MY GOD YOU'RE BEAUTIFUL WITHOUT YOUR GLASSES. COME HERE I'M GONNA KISS YOU LIKE THEY DO IN THE MOVIES'. At which point he pulls her to his chest, sways a bit to build up the required momentum, and flings her over his arm Valentino fashion. They overbalance and fall to the floor, which doesn't bother Jenkins unduly since he is on top of the situation. Without further ado he covers her with kisses.

'Well, you could call them kisses,' said Charlotte recoiling in horror at the memory 'if you were feeling generous. I wasn't. My dress was covered with saliva. I hate tongue sarnies.'

One must sympathise, as no doubt you will appreciate if your Jenkins is still at the slobbery stage. And if he is, do not despair. Things can only get better.

Sex Three: Nocturne in Flock

If Music Be The Food Of Love, Where's The Nearest Takeaway?

Once Jenkins has had a few trial runs with girls, he decides that sex is one thing, romance is quite another. Thereafter he doesn't fall in love, he plummets. In fact his attitude to the whole topic is like his attitude to illness: a graze is cissy, a gash is great.

This is wonderful, you may think, the first encouraging news you've read. Sorry, sister, but not so fast with the euphoria. As per usual Jenkins doesn't quite know where to stop. For instance, a friend of mine who was celebrating her 21st birthday recently answered her doorbell to discover a florist hidden under 21 red roses, 21 stems of jasmine and 21 miniature orange trees. When she had dug the delivery man out she asked him for the card, eagerly tore it open and instantly uttered a horrified gasp of astonishment.

'Who are they from?' said a voice behind her.

'J-Jenkins,' she said miserably.

'Ah, ha! So you won't be wanting the ring after all,' exclaimed her fiancé of ten minutes as he made his way out of her life.

In other words there may be times when you wish that the Jenkins who worships from afar would do so from even further. Another universe, for preference.

From Jenkins's point of view, the real problem is that you are a woman. It is your very femininity that disturbs him, throwing his otherwise orderly life into chaos. Strange emotions are coursing through his veins, and it makes him feel frightfully uncomfortable. After all, he probably hasn't had a good emotional worry for years and he has to be given time to decide whether he is in love, or the sensation is actually a symptom of something less serious like appendicitis. One Jenkins I know recently described falling in love as something akin to having a multiple birth without being warned. He didn't say whether he drew his analogy from the mother's point of view or the child's but you catch his drift, I imagine. Whereas women, he went on to inform me, find falling in love about as difficult as falling off a log, as far as he could see. Which just proves how insensitive we females are, I suppose.

Incidentally, it is worth remembering that though certain events in Jenkins's life may seem nothing more than normal to you, he sees things in quite a different light. Everything he does for the first time is a lunge forward in the progress of mankind. Thus the first time he gets a job, catches influenza or falls in love is, he is sure, the first time that this has happened in the history of the human race, a mini miracle which is probably destined to be the eighth wonder of the world. Never smirk at his delight when something like this has occurred, just smile encouragingly. Furthermore, should he ever tell you that you have no idea of the trouble you have caused by existing on the same planet and threatens to take the matter up with your parents, don't upstage him by saying you are sure they didn't have him in mind when you were conceived: he won't believe you, he'll just feel insecure and sulk. Oh, and for goodness sake, never imply by thought or word or deed that he might be a smidgen immature when it comes to emotion. Just encourage him. Go on, it's worth a try.

Frailty Thy Name Is Henrietta

The tragedy of Jenkins is that the moment his feelings are engaged his tongue gets twisted and he is totally unable to tell the girl of his dreams about his passion. Instead he idolises, nay, deifies her. She's up there on a pedestal and he's down here being a grub, and he seems to almost like it that way. Destiny dictates, therefore, that no union shall be achieved until the goddess pitches off her plinth and into his lap. One way of looking at this is to say that the poor boy is painfully shy. Another view, circulated by cynics and malefactors, is that Jenkins is congenitally lazy.

So if you are in love with your Jenkins, and have a reasonably hot tip that the feeling could be made mutual, start planning your strategy now. There is not a moment to lose . . . Unless of course you aren't crazy about having children, in which case you can leave it to him to make the first move without worrying whether he'll get round to doing anything before you get round to the menopause.

Reading the Signs

If you are going to plan any sort of campaign, be it military or advertising in nature, it is generally deemed a good idea to recce the territory before you wade in with your size five wellies on. If you don't, you stand a good chance of encountering disaster.

The most important thing to do to start with is to learn to read the signs that Jenkins is making. I am afraid you will not be terrifically happy with this piece of advice, as more likely than not you will be totally bemused by all his signals. He might throw you the odd crumb of conversation every now and then, even grace you with a smile from time to time, but this is scant incentive to turn yourself into Mata Hari. In fact if Jenkins is still using the general all purpose form of address when talking to you, by which I mean he never uses your name but starts a conversation with '. . . er . . .' you probably think you have about as much chance of success as a donkey at the Grand National.

But bear up! As a general rule of thumb, the more he likes you the more unpleasant he will be. It is only if he is being super-gallant that you need to worry, especially if you are any sort of heiress. The nastiness is actually a sort of test: can you love him with his warts on, as it were. So if he is very free with his insults and can never think of anything to say save 'Crumbs, you look ropey today, and you ought to do something about your mascara you've got pin striped cheeks,' for heavens sake don't rush off to the bunkers for a quick blub. This is his way of saying usually he thinks you look scrummy and he doesn't like to see you letting yourself down. Jenkins is never free with his compliments at the best of times and indeed I know of one who told his bride she looked awful in white even before they got out of the church, so the sooner you get used to his brusqueness the better off you'll be.

But you must not let him think that you are too tough. A friend of mine happily met insult with insult and had practically forgotten she was in love at all until one day young Jenkins, charming as ever, said 'My God, you look even worse today. Want me to ring for an ambulance, eh?' At which point she burst into tears. In a flash, Jenkins was at her side, covering her with kisses and apologies. He was sympathetic when she told him about the death of her goldfish which was the cause of her sensitivity and the migraine which was the cause of her pallor and even when she asked him to kiss her more quietly since every little smooch was as a hatchet blow to her cerebellum he seemed to understand. He had been frightened to approach her before, you see, as she seemed much too good at keeping the upper hand. And as Jenkins is a timid creature, you know, he will never embark on a venture unless he is sure of a route in his favour.

Oh, and before you dismiss Jenkins's rudeness as tangible evidence that he is a bore, do remember the old hang-up about cissyness. In the very early stages of love he has to try to find a way to stand out from the crowd without appearing to be wet. Hence the nastiness.

Silly? Yes. Counter-productive? More often than not. Bizarre? Absolutely. But then we are talking about Jenkins, if you recall.

Tracking The Beast

In the early stages of the campaign it is as well to stick like glue to the old Victorian maxim and don't speak until you are spoken to if you can possibly help it. I know that this isn't exactly a thrilling plan of action, but in reality it is a sort of negative sortie into enemy territory. Jenkins has been led to believe that women never stop talking and this bothers him. After all, when a chap is scripting the seduction scene to end all seduction scenes, he likes to feel that he will be able to get a word in sideways. Anyway, the silence will add a veil of mystery to all the other things you are wearing, and you will find that you have become an enigma, like all the other famous heroines devised by men for their own delight.

Remember that Jenkins is a credulous fellow and if other men tell him women are alright if you can't afford a hot water bottle, but you wouldn't want them on top of a hangover, he believes them. His faith is rather touching really, sort of blind and naïve, almost like a child who believes in fairies. Especially when you consider that few of his cronies have been within spitting distance of a woman in a nightie let alone had one on top of a hangover or anything else. So you see, your being taciturn will combat these vicious rumours and if you keep it up for long enough, he will soon be panting to hear your views on everything from Descartes to durex.

There is a catch to this, though. When you do finally open your mouth, it had better be to let a 22 carat showstopper comment out. 'Could you tell me the time?' is not the sort of conversational gambit we are looking for here, unless of course your Jenkins has joined the Boys in Blue.

And don't overdo the silence bit, either. After all you don't want him to think you cannot speak at all. Jenkins has a melodramatic explanation for most things and if he assumes you are a deaf-mute he will shy off pronto; he knows his father is looking for a good healthy daughter-in-law to keep the line alive.

The real trick is to be able to fascinate everyone in sight with your intelligence, exuberance and general all-round sense of fun and then cover yourself in wordless confusion when he joins the conversation. It is also a good idea to transmit the glad news that you are a jolly sensible sort of girl. Any quivering of the lips on subjects other than the monarchy or animals will indicate that you are neurotic and therefore to be avoided like the bubonic plague. Also, if by some caprice of fate you have been blighted with too much intelligence keep it quiet. He doesn't want to know if you are as informed about the Campaign for Nuclear Disarmament as you are about Point-to-Points. He intends to be master of any situation and a brainy female is more threatening to his power base than a

Communist government. Time enough to flash your philosophy around after you have met his mum, by which time you will feel as though you have had a lobotomy anyway, and won't have two words to string together and call your own.

Going In For The Kill

Quite how long this preliminary argy-bargy goes on depends on you. Personally, I can't stand all this shrinking violet stuff much more than a month before I start to worry that I'm next in line for an attack of cerebral greenfly. Really impetuous types have been known to end the first stage of the game after a week or two, and launch themselves literally headlong into the next phase. There are several ways of doing this, some of which are altogether too extreme for me.

Take the example of my good friend Emma, who distinguished herself by pitching her lissom little body directly into her Jenkins's ski path thereby causing him to break her arm and bring about the sudden demise of his own left ski. The medical bills were shocking since there is no NHS in Switzerland and the silly child had forgotten her insurance chit. Her black eye, which was outrageous, frightened children for weeks, but she achieved her goal; he took her out to dinner.

Fortunately for the Jenkinses of this world this course of action is not open to us most of the year, and somehow dry ski-slopes just don't have the same éclat. So if you want to take drastic action you'll have to come up with an alternative plan for yourself. A word of warning before you do . . .

Try not to put yourself in a position whereby you end up permanently disfigured. Old Emma is one of the stalwarts of our sex, and hardier than most, and for frailer creatures physical daring is dangerous.

After all, there is a danger that he may turn out not to be worth the plaster you've got your limb in.

The object of the operation at this moment is simply to put him into the position where he feels it is his duty to spend some time with you, rather than perpetrate an act of suicidal folly which might put the mockers on your possibly promising career. Also bear in mind that he views the gentle sex with the deepest suspicion, and likes to think that he got along without them pretty well as a youth, so he ought to be able to get along without them in his dotage as well. Yes, I know that this is a direct contradiction to his romantic leanings, but that is the nature of the beast, and that, is also that, as Christopher Robin would say.

Mind you, the amount of emotional and physical colateral a girl has to put up before Jenkins feel that his conquest is assured and makes a move himself is quite extraordinary. One girl I know gave increasingly heavy hints to the object of her desires for a year or more. She sent him a barely anonymous Valentine, a perfectly sweet birthday present in the form of a wing-mirror he coveted for his motor-bike and finally a downright blatant Christmas present: a bottle of champagne accompanied by a card bearing the legend 'a present shared is a pleasure doubled'. And absolutely nothing happened at all. Her confidence ebbed ever lower.

Then one night she gave him a lift home after a party and invited herself in to make the coffee. He was totally plastered and she was far from sober herself, so she ended up making breakfast as well. The next day in that churningly sickening way new lovers have, she asked when he had first noticed that she quite liked him.

'Oh, when you took my shirt off, I think,' came the casual reply.

'But what about the Valentine and the wing-mirror

Going in for the kill – directly into Jenkins's ski path

and the champagne?' she wailed, looked for all the world as though she had just lost a fight with a wet fish.

'Oh, *them*,' he said in an offhand sort of way. 'I just thought they were the kind of thing that some girls did.'

Which once again illustrates the fact that sex-education at Public School leaves an awful lot to be desired.

Now, there might be those among you who feel that this particular friend of mine played even faster and looser than the energetic Emma, and in some ways I am bound to agree with you. On the other hand, as she points out herself, at least she and her Jenkins knew each other fairly well before they went out together for the first time, and that is an advantage not to be sneezed at, as you will soon discover.

The Tête à Tête, Or How to Survive a Head-on Collision

If and when Jenkins finally asks you out to dinner, you will probably feel very pleased with yourself and think you are progressing wonderfully. Well you are, actually, and not even this voice of doom is going to deny you that little triumph. Please don't let it go to your head though, for you are now at the top of the very slippery slope and though it could be a superb slalom, the first evening you spend alone with him is pretty much the Jenkins equivalent of trial by ordeal.

The first thing to be aware of is timing. For goodness sake be ready when he arrives. It was all very well keeping gentlemen waiting when the Mitfords were in charge of love in this cold climate, but then they didn't detain their suitors in an icy drawing room festooned with their flatmates freshly laundered knicky-knacky-knoos. They didn't have flatmates, either, come to that, and however close two girls maybe, Jenkins is only mortal and not above breaking up the happy home, if you see what I mean.

The other reason for prompt attention to Jenkins when he arrives is his own obsession with precision timing which dates back to his school-days, bowel-movements and so on. So if he has told you to be ready at 8, *be* ready at 8 just this once, or you'll have lost ground before you leave the starting gate.

Oh, and don't stint yourself on the preparations, either. Splosh on the scent and dress up to the hilt if the spirit moves you. He may well mistake the subtle perfume for fly-spray and wonder how you can walk under all those frills, but at least it will give you some confidence. Anyway, he'll probably appreciate it secretly especially if he's new to the wining and dining game, as he'll doubtless take you to a restaurant recommended by his father and won't want to let the family side dowm.

Apart from these very general guidelines, there is little I can say to help you now, as *I've* never met the fellow. So basically you're on your own, kid, at least for the duration of the meal. Just remember the golden rules for survival in the close combat zone of the dinner table. These are as follows: – laugh at his jokes, keep off blood sports if you are anti, poetry if you are pro and for goodness sake don't start talking about astrology, this is no time to get personal.

Most importantly, don't have any suggestions to make about the wine. If you do, he'll think you are a woman of the world or a vamp and may well conclude that you are the self-appointed dessert course and you could end up going to bed hungry. All in all, concentrate on being the English rose in full bloom, and once he's decided if he's bird or bee, everything in the garden should be lovely.

Oh For Some Etchings

Whether your mother'd like it or not, when all goes well with the jolly discourse over supper, it is likely to lead to a night-time course of quite a different order. Unfortunately for you if this seems like your cue for letting your hair down, you've jumped an act or two. Sex is a dicey business at the best of times and with Jenkins it can all too often seem that the dice are loaded against you.

This is particularly true if your spring-board to the mattress is the offer of a cup of coffee back at his place, as this almost inevitably means you are going to be even more alone than you were in the restaurant. What could be better, you might ask? A darkened crowded room, my dear, is the unhelpful reply. You see Jenkins is happier to move to the sofa from the dance floor as that way fewer questions have to be asked and the music is so loud that all decisions take on the aura of being mutual. Quite apart from the fact that at a party everyone is doing more or less the same sort of thing and you know how Jenkins likes to feel that he is One of The Boys. For that reason, it is a relatively short step from dancing cheek to cheek to paying lipservice to mine host for the state of his duvet.

In the drawing room the whole business is a lot trickier, and the bigger the room the trickier the business. If there is central heating you really do have a problem – you don't even have the excuse of snuggling up to the fire as a sort of modest halfway house to snuggling up to something more likely to respond to your attention, like the dog. If there isn't even a dog, then I honestly do pity you. If you can get the hound on your side, you see, you are practically home and dry, for Jenkins always likes a second opinion, and there is nothing so reassuring to him as the approval of the family's pet girl-eater. Without it he may decide not to take any risks at all, his own judgement being somewhat untried.

One of the best places to go through all the tedious preliminaries in the days of yore used to be the box-room. There was always a good excuse to get in there because you could ask to see the train set. Nowadays people tend to keep lodgers in this conveniently tiny place instead of little Hornby station masters, so the whole ploy loses its charm. I don't for a moment suggest that you ask if you can go and see the lodger instead, either. You may be an exhibitionist by nature, but Jenkins most definitely isn't, and in his book two's company, three's positively pornographic.

So you will inevitably find yourself in the next best thing to Wembly stadium with a carpet where standard lamps double as floodlights and you and the man seem to have been picked as opposing goalies. It seems that the only solution is to kick an own-goal somehow, and hope he'll rush over and congratulate you as though you had just won the UEFA cup for his team.

It would help if Jenkins hadn't chosen this moment to show what a gentleman he can be. A virtuoso display of good breeding is rather chastening when your own thoughts are about as lady-like as Jezebel. Especially when he's probably worrying about you being someone else's sister again, and imagining that your brother is built like Goliath. The enthusiastic Emma has been known to cut the room down to a more manageable size by suggesting a gentle game of musical chairs, to promote the party mood, as it were. She got away with it too, or so she tells me. She is the most dreadful braggart. But this is not a universally acceptable way of dealing with the situation, especially if one or more of the chairs is a Chesterfield. It is also pretty difficult to play this game when there are only two people as there is no-one to turn the music off. If you honestly imagine that this is the sort of thing you can see yourself doing, you will have to ask her to supply the technical details – there are times when Emma and I disagree about acceptable cunning, and this is one of them. Anyway, if the poor fellow is expected to lumber vast great family heirlooms about the place in the wee small hours of the morning, I don't think he would be in a fit state to raise much enthusiasm for any other games for some considerable time.

The only thing to do, I think, is to pray for fortitude in the form of a stiff brandy, and feign temporary deafness or pretend to lose your voice. This way you can edge closer in the interests of easier communication thereby starting to close the gulf between you without looking totally brazen. And don't rush things, let nature take its course. Jenkins is working through the situation in his own indefatigable way, and before any progress can be made at all there are one or two little matters that this born-again Gentil Knight has to resolve for himself.

You can of course help him a bit. Pay close attention to what he has to say. Whenever he clears his throat, look as though you are sure he's about to drop a pearl of wisdom, and you are determined to appreciate it.

This will encourage him greatly, and make him think that you are a sympathetic sort. Of course his utterances will be more or less inconsequential like 'Do you like Bob Dylan?' but do not take them lightly. If you give the wrong answer you could well find yourself with a pre-paid taxi-ride to your doom. Heroes are nothing to be scoffed at, you know, and this is no time to murmur sweetly that you have never heard of the gentleman in question.

It is when he says 'er . . . um . . . are you?' and

leaves the air vacant for possession that you really have to be on your metal. Failure at this stage is fatal, if you are planning to turn Him'n'Me into Us. So give him a moment or two to try to finish the sentence, and if he has resorted to making gurgling noises and whistling, look determinedly at your shoes and say 'yes'. A prolonged silence will inevitably ensue but don't spoil the moment by yelling 'I said YES' as though you expected the earth to jump off its axis there and then. Try to keep your counsel. For you have just painlessly disposed of the sticky subject of contraception and are under starter's orders for a quick trot round the etchings.

By the way, there is absolutely no point in taking a feminist stand over this or any other issue with young Jenkins. Resign from your consciousness raising group instead, and make life a little easier for yourself. Because once they realise who you've chosen to dump your heart on this time you'll get no end of flak from the sisters, and Jenkins won't be overly polite about *them* either. Any attempt to make them co-exist harmoniously in different corners of your life is doomed to failure and as pig-in-the-middle it will be you who goes hurtling off in hot pursuit of a cheap psychiatrist and not them!

In other words, the responsibility for ensuring that the sound of little footsteps does not echo in your ears unscheduled is yours. As I pointed out earlier, Jenkins is a romantic at heart, and therefore making love bears precisely no relation to making babies as far as he can see. Ladies and their unfortunate innards hold no fascination for him, abiding though his passion for his own bowels may be. Furthermore if you aren't too embarrassed to talk about your natural role in life, you jolly well should be, because Jenkins finds the whole subject utterly mortifying. Fatherhood is something he will contemplate only after consulting his accountant, and that will be some time after somebody has married him.

Which is not to say that he won't do the decent thing if you are goofy enough to go into mass production by accident. Of course he will. He has been well brought up and would consider it a duty to give the child his name. But in this day and age it is considered quite sufficient for the bride's mother to cry at the wedding without the groom sobbing into his morning coat as well.

Meanwhile, back to the etchings . . . Once these and other forms of conversational foreplay are dispensed with it will probably be time to give your candid opinion on the colour scheme he has chosen for his own room. If you don't know by now that this is a rhetorical question, I can only assume that you are a slow learner, for at this juncture Jenkins tends to act in much the same way as any other bloke, so they say. Should you feel that you really must keep the conversation razzing along for a while, then this is the time to say that it has ever been your dearest wish to have the exact same paper in your own room, but you have always been prevented from doing so by thinking that it might be a little harsh to wake up to. Play your cards right and you could shortly be watching the sunrise over one of Osbourne and Little's finest flocks.

That Dreadful Morning After Feeling

Eight hours or so after your initial doubts about interior decoration one can safely assume that you and Jenkins have become a lot closer. Unfortunately this does not immediately imply that you know each other a lot better. So don't start flinging endearments around the place as though you were lovers or something, because that thought will not yet have occurred to Jenkins, and indeed, it may never do so. Which means that words like 'Darling, Sweetness, and Honey' will hit him on the temple like one of Dennis Lillie's best, and you might never be invited back for the second test. One girl's endearments are another man's crumpled reputation, and you know how Jenkins feels about being soppy. Of course, this works both ways. When he starts referring to you as 'my old tart' you may not like it, but at least you will know that you are held in high esteem and have made some sort of impact on his life.

Oh, and I do hope that you realise that this is the worst moment in the evolution of the universe to start saying things like 'I love you'. Jenkins is easily shocked and you don't want him to get the impression that you are one of the flighty sort who wear their hearts on their sleeves.

In fact I ought to tell you that the fully fledged Jenkins is allergic to those three little words. It is as though they were a death knell in his ears. Goodness knows why. Perhaps he thinks they imply some sort of commitment and he has not yet learned that Breach of Promise is no longer a Civil Offence. Whatever the reason for this strange phobia Jenkins will go to absurd lengths to avoid admitting that he has the capacity for affection at all. Witness the conversation between my good friend Fiona and the Light In Her Life.

'Oh, darling,' she murmured as she surveyed Wales from a high pre-Cambrian peak, 'Isn't this perfect?'

'Well, yes,' he agreed. 'Look Fi, there's something I have to tell you.'

'Yes?'

'I just feel you ought to know . . . I don't want to give you the wrong impression or anything . . . but the fact is I don't love you . . . it's nothing personal you understand . . . I don't even love me . . . fact is, I don't know what love *is*.'

'I know, darling, I know,' she told him soothingly. 'After all, you have been giving me weekly bulletins about this for the last three years or so.'

'Just making sure.'

'Only Jenkins, I sometimes wonder, I mean, we have been living together for two of those years now, and I'd hate you to think I was cramping your style. Shouldn't you be off smoking the Princess Charming of your life out of her hidden den? You're not getting any younger you know, and I'd hate you to leave it too late.'

'Hey, look, I didn't say I wasn't fond of you, you know. You haven't gone off me have you?'

Fiona smiled an enigmatic smile and looked down on the land of Glendwr even more benignly, or at least she says she did. Which ought to bring home the message about love talk very firmly. If Fiona, who is no cringing Lily won't be drawn after three years, you'd be well advised to keep your mouth firmly closed after just one night.

In fact quite the best thing you can do after a perfunctory breakfast is dematerialise. Melt away like the morning dew that Wodehouse was so fond of. And resist the temptation of buying a new vase on the way home. Romantic though he may like to think he is, Jenkins will be much too busy trying to work out whether he has just had a dream or a nightmare to be wandering in and out of flower shops like a man demented.

Obviously you'll be anxious to know what he is thinking in the afterglow, and the next few days may very well be dark ones for you. But don't fret: they'll be even worse for Jenkins – pitch-black, in all probability. The emotions that were tickling through his brains before will have turned into a torrent, the mere thought of you will bring him out in a monsoon-like sweat and he will probably already be blaming you for the cardiac arrest he feels sure is imminent.

Don't call him, though. Let him make contact with you. If he doesn't, make discreet enquiries and decide for yourself whether to send for Christian Barnard or blacken his name as a cur, a fool and an abuser of poor gentle womanhood.

If he does, spoil yourself. Have a smirk and a new dress. You might even lash out on a new pair of shoes if you like, because by now, you really are doing rather well.

Sex Four: A Few Country Reels

Courting Trouble

Though you are now doing thrillingly well, and in many ways have become what the bookies call an odds-on favourite instead of a rank outsider, you haven't won the race yet. In fact you will shortly be among those who may make you feel even ranker an outsider than before. Or, to put it another way, you may have a decisive victory to your credit, but there's still a war on, lady.

Going Behind The Lines

Oh, dear, this is a nasty bit, and I do have a nagging suspicion that you are radically unprepared for it as well. I mean, I have tried to warn you that Jenkins, unlike the cat, never walks alone; but maybe not strongly enough. Still, there is an argument for concentrating on one individual at a time, and it does help you prepare for taking on the hordes which will form the most serious opposition that you have faced so far. Honestly, when you think about it, you'll see that Hercules got off lightly.

The thing is, if Jenkins is toying with the idea of cleaving you to his bossom he will expect you first of all to cleave to the bosom of his friends as well – metaphorically speaking of course. If they don't like you or accept you then, sooner or later, Jenkins will find his passion has cooled too. This is not because he is weak or biddable either. If he were, you could at last cheer yourself with the thought that you wouldn't want to spend your life with a torrential drip anyway. No, the brutal truth is that if it comes to a toss up between eternal bliss with you and severance from his chums, it's heads they win, tails you lose. So it's up to you to make sure it never comes to that, unless you've got your own supply of double sided coins.

Mind you, Jenkins will want you to become one of his gang. I mean, he won't start off being on the other side, because after all he is probably 'fond' of you by now. Nevertheless, don't expect him to cavort around wearing his heart on his sleeve with your name copper-plated through the middle of it because he won't. To be liquidisingly honest, when you are first exposed to his friends *en masse* your name may not come into it at all.

This stage of the proceedings floored even the extraordinary Emma. Somewhat surprisingly, all her tactics had worked beautifully, even to the extent that her Jenkins happily thought he had done all the chasing and referred to her as Emma the Enigma. Quite what this teaches us about her beloved's powers of observation I wouldn't care to say, but I have given Emma the name of a good optician. Despite his apparent myopia, he and Emma were in the middle of living happily ever after until he gave a drinks party.

Poor Emma. She had spent weeks making natty little cheese straws, days making witty little dips and hours de-sogging those round biscuit things that you dip in with, which always come fresh – and limp – from the packet. At seven thirty, the door-bell began to ring. Jenkins was busy emptying the rest of the drinks cabinet into the punch bowl to get the colour right so Emma went to answer the door. She still had her pinnie on, which may have accounted for the initial reaction of the first guest, but it certainly didn't leave the later ones with any excuse. Or at least it shouldn't have.

'It was just ultra-horrid,' she told me the next day, sobbing so prolifically into the phone I though she might get electrocuted and waited desperately for a pause in her flow so I could tell her to go and put her wellies on and earth herself just in case.

'The first person who came in took one look at me, grunted and proffered his overcoat. I only took it because I couldn't think of anything else to do and the next thing I knew, everyone was treating me like I was the hired help or hat-check girl or whatever it is they have in Manhattan. The worst thing was that nobody talked to me,' which was a blow indeed for Emma, who is the gregarious sort. 'Then, when we went to supper everyone looked at me as though I should have been serving it instead of eating it. I felt as if I was contagious, or something.'

'Sounds like that's just what you weren't, dear, at least on the popularity stakes,' I said, which wasn't very kind of me, I admit. Well, I had been listening uninterrupted for about a year: the above is the abridged version.

'Pah,' retorted Emma. 'You just don't understand. Jenkins didn't introduce me to anyone.'

That's the annoying thing about Emma: she has a very Jenkins-like capacity to believe that she's the only person ever to have experienced anything. Heaven help us when she has her first baby – she's sure to expect Darwin to come back and re-write the theory of evolution. In fact knowing her, she'll probably arrange it. But that's neither here nor there as far as you're concerned, except to say that actually I *did* understand how she felt and so do a good many others. Most seasoned campaigners have been through the non-introduction hoop, which means that once again though I can't actually make it less likely to happen, I can at least encourage you not to take it personally.

There are two reasons for this behaviour and the first is not unconnected with the old monster cissy-ness. If Jenkins were to introduce you by name, rank and number he'd say 'Hello, Smythie, I don't think you've met Blah my girlfriend,' which would make life very much easier for you, especially if you are the sort of girl who won't approach anyone until you are introduced on the grounds that you shouldn't speak to strangers. He can't do that though, because if he did, he would by implication be admitting some emotional attachment and emotional attachments are cissy; and you can probably guess the rest.

The second is even less logical, even harder to understand and absolutely impossible to sympathise with. It is rooted in Jenkins's outlook on the world. As long as he can remember it has been populated with his schoolfriends, who all know each other – and him – like the backs of their hands. This means that he expects them to know how he feels about you despite the fact that he hasn't worked it out himself yet and *they* have no previous data to go on. Another part of this is that if he is sufficiently used to having you around to let you meet his friends, he's probably forgotten you don't know them and therefore feels introductions to be superfluous. It's that old double-think again: one of the myriad wonders of the public school world.

I hope I have now illustrated that when Jenkins takes you behind his lines, he may not actually be against you, but he isn't exactly the best man alive at providing covering fire. So the only thing that you can do to promote your own survival is to walk in zig-zags, as it were. I'm not exactly sure of the military

Nobody talked to me

rationalisation for this, but sure as eggs, pardner, it seemed to work for Clint Eastwood.

Infiltrating The Enemy

A nifty way of staking your claim in the Jenkins camp is to win over the other occupants of the Women's Quarters. I know that this will seem a horribly daunting prospect at first, because despite the rise of feminism and so on, no feeling of solidarity is instantly discernible and as Jessica once said, 'those so called ladies can behave in the most ungentlemanly way, on occasion.' She turns a neat epigram, does Jessica, but I sometimes wonder if it won't get her into trouble one of these days.

Oh, and before you recoil in horror, do remember that we are all sisters under the skin, clichéd though the sentiment may be. I've been on both sides of this particular fence now, and I will say with my hand on my heart that though there are several aspects of the hostility which are quite unpraiseworthy, there is one which is positively useful: if you can't cope with Jenkins's friends' consorts, you haven't a prayer with the females in his family and at least you'll be frightened off in time to avoid actually being eaten alive.

Do also cling to the knowledge that even in this day and age, women are still the power behind the throne, even if they are fearfully upfront almost everywhere else. In other words, if the girls are on your side, there's a hot chance that they'll help win the boys over too.

Try to discover who was the last interloper before you and ingratiate yourself sickeningly with her. Quite how you'll find out who she is I'm not sure – it'll be a little initiative test for you. Naturally, it's no good applying to Jenkins for help, since he's unlikely to remember. Usually intelligent guesswork will see you through. There is frequently an unspoken pecking order and the last in line will be she who makes the least or the most noise, depending on the nature of the group.*

Once the bond is made with the other girl, however tenuously, it is wise to sit back and listen for a while. You're bound to learn something interesting. For instance, when I was a Novitiate myself, my Sister Superior was moved to inform me that I really 'shouldn't show you have different opinions from Jenkins in public, you know. At least not yet. People'll get the idea that you are brainy or something, and that will never do. Quite apart from the fact that it unsettles the poor boy. I've known him for years and I can tell.'

I was fascinated by this statement for a while, not to say flummoxed and non-plussed but I am happy to say that she and I are now the very greatest of friends, and even, when in our cups, have laughed about this iffie moment in our acquaintance.

The great thing about infiltrating the enemy like this, is that it acts as a barometer which will tell you whether your stock is falling or rising. If it is the former, your new found friend will be becoming increasingly cool, if it is the latter, she will rapidly warm towards you. It may seem uncomfortably like riding a weather-vane for a bit, but at least you are in the eye of the wind.

When you are finally accepted, and the various trials by cocktail parties have proved that you are not a witch, a profiteer or worse, you will 'know by a sign,' as one always does at times of high destiny. It will happen thus; you will be invited for tea or something a little more congenial by one or more of

* A swift refresher course of the chapter in T. H. White's Sword in The Stone where Wart becomes a bird for a night might be jolly useful here.

the other girls and it will be made abundantly clear to you that Jenkins is not on the guest list too. As the ice chinks nervously against the glass someone will clear her throat and say something like '*Do* you remember what we said about poor Henrietta when we first met her. God, we were horrid, weren't we, and *so* wrong!' You will then hear just how nasty they were about you and is a signal for everyone to get terribly jolly and tell you what a relief you have turned out to be.

At last all will become clear to you. The other girls were filthy towards you because in the past every female Jenkins has been remotely connected with has been a forty-two carat tart, lemon, or something unmentionable. Indeed, they will tell you, they had all become frightened that he was making a habit out of getting his heart broken and needed to be saved from himself, he was so vulnerable, poor wee lamb.

The funniest thing about this distinctly peculiar line of thought is that after a while you will feel exactly the same way about any unattached male member of the clan. Please don't ask me why – it's probably got something to do with symbiosis or another of those gorgeous, magic-sounding scientific processes – I only know it happens, that's all. When it's your turn to undergo the sea-change and check out new young hopefulettes, do remember how awkward it was on the other side of the fence, in no-woman's-land.

Don't Frighten The Horses

It has long been acknowledged in this handbook that in many ways the female constitution is stronger than that of Homos Jenkinsus. In no case is this so true as when an alien female encroaches the purlieus of Jenkinsland and wins the support of the women already resident. This means that even when all the other girls are backing Britannia in the form of you, you must skip only the lightest fandango of joy. More raucous celebrations will have the men yelling 'Plot, plot' as though you were a direct descendant of G. Fawkes Esq., and Jenkins will help them build the bonfire out of sheer force of habit.

You have now reached one of the most delicate balances of your unmarried life with Jenkins and even the slightest whisper too many could tip the scales against you, so hush, hush, breathe not a word. Let others do the work for you.

Oh and when I say not a word, for heaven's sake don't take me too literally. I've explained before about the melodramatic tendency of the species, and even though Jenkins may have discovered you're not a deaf mute, you don't want to worry his friends. You know how influential they can be. The best thing is to decide what role you are going to play, write yourself a few juicy lines and stick to the script. That way you can be pretty sure that you won't do anything shocking, which is useful because unpredictable women give Jenkins's friends the heebie-jeebies. Witness the sad tale of Camilla, that most accommodating of secretaries with the film-directoring boss.

Some time after the episode with the boeuf et champignons en croute, Camilla and the gourmet Jenkins noticed that they were wildly attracted to each other. In telling us this she didn't exactly resemble the boys who took the news from Ghent to Aix since we'd all noticed weeks before, and put the young lovers' slowness down to pressure of work. Thus we were very relieved when that great Busby Berkeley on high caught the pair in centre set and commanded the celestial camera crew to turn over, cut and print. We didn't even mind much that love blinded her and she saw none of her old friends for a couple of months. However, when she reappeared, exhausted, bedraggled and woebegone we did feel a little concerned as we poured the tea and sympathy. It's not pleasant to see a good girl brought down, especially one as resilient as she.

What had happened? What had gone wrong? Where was Jenkins? We chorused agog. The child just hung her head, numbed and terribly confused.

It was a pitiful sight, and before very long the mob of her trusted friends were in the mood to lynch someone, preferably the Jenkins in her life, good and proper.

I think in retrospect she must have sensed our mood and stepped in to save him from the gallows. She knew that hell doth have a fury worse than that of a woman scorned: the corporate fury of the friends of the slighted damsel.

'Oh, it was all my fault,' she began unpromisingly. The rest of us sat down, pursed our lips and waited. 'It was alright when we were with friends from the business, you know, admen, photographers, actors and so on. I mean you're all equal with those sort of people. Well, alright, you're all equal if you've got enough talent and money. But it was his old school friends, his *real* friends I s'pose that got me.'

A frisson of worry shimmied down the backs of her audience swiftly followed by a sense of *déjà vu*. It was a bit like a Smokers Anonymous class when someone admits to having had an illicit ciggie. We all braced ourselves in an attempt not to look disapproving.

'Have you ever *been* to one of those gatherings? Yes? Then you'll know all about it. At first I thought it was the women who were against me, but then I realised they were all human really. So I started to try to be friendly to the men, only they all looked at me as though Jenkins was in the porn-movie business and I was his only star. So I got frightened and kind of clung to him a bit. Not physically. Just you know, made sure he was within reach. Then he told me they all thought I was difficult so I tried to make an effort again and it seemed to be going so well that I gave a couple of them a kiss goodbye and that was it. Jenkins said I was a neurotic trollop and bang!' At which point she began to sob hysterically.

'Oh dear,' clucked her sister Amy. 'She frightened the horses.'

Camilla herself then assumed an expression not unlike that worn by a startled mare and said 'What'?

'It doesn't matter what you do in private, but don't do it in public and frighten the horses,' explained Amy, misquoting madly.

'Oh I see,' lied her sister.

We explained to her that in this instance for 'horse' one should read Jenkins, but it didn't seem to help. In case you are in the same sort of dilemma, allow me to interpret these oracular pronouncements.

Jenkinses, like the horse, are frightened by any behaviour that runs counter to the norm, and Camilla had committed a fatal mistake in not establishing a normal *modus operandi* to begin with, which is a real puzzle to me since she is usually the very normalest of girls. Now, since big butchie types don't readily admit that a girl has reduced them to the nail-biting stage, mentally speaking, they cover up by pouring scorn and derision on her head behind her back, if you can grasp my meaning. The consequence of which was that Jenkins showed her the door.

But whence comes this disturbing cowardice in the Public School hunk? Can't you guess? From school, nit! It probably goes back to the days when they all united, pack-like, against some passing common foe.

Poor old Camilla, her extraordinary behaviour seemed to be threatening the unity of the pack so they threw her out like an unwanted joker; an ignominious fate for anyone.

Therefore, you seeker after the Jenkins, profit by her mistakes. Keep a low profile and let the girls be your press agents. With any luck they'll manage to convince the men that when you and Jenkins are as one, they won't be losing a fellow hound so much as gaining a brace of cubs, given time.

Share And Share Alike

Although it's jolly nice being one of the in-crowd when you finally make it, you may come to believe that it can have its drawbacks. For example whenever you're at home, the crowd always seems to be around, and it can be terribly difficult to get an evening alone with Jenkins. Indeed, I know one girl who became so fed up with having constantly to perform the five loaves and two fishes trick with a romantic TV dinner for two that when she heard Waterloo Station was going to be renovated she put in a bid for the old brass plaque that commemorated the site of a war-time soup kitchen; she wanted it for her own kitchen door. She didn't get it, which is just as well really, since she'd probably only have encouraged even more visitors.

The worst thing about it is that once you are part of an established couple, all Jenkins friends assume that the lovey-dovey bit is over and you'll be glad of a visit from someone to break the humdrum monotony of your lives. This applies particularly to unencumbered Jenkinses for two reasons a) they want your beloved's advice about their pursuit of happiness since he's obviously an expert to have caught a champion greatlookinbottlewashinshirtpressin woman like and b) they feel it unnatural that a man, or indeed a human being, who has been brought up to share a house with umpteen others for 38 weeks a year can possibly feel at home in a place less populated. The only thing to look forward to is the school holidays, when maybe they'll feel able to leave you alone.

The flip side of this particular coin is even more frustrating. If, for some bizarre reason – a celebration like a birthday or an anniversary or something – you and Jenkins decline an invitation, and hint that you want to be alone, everyone who knows and loves you will fly into a panic. The only reason they can think of for any two people wanting to be alone all evening is to have a good row. Before you know it the bush telegraph will be transmitting notes of commiseration and offers of spare rooms. It's no good feigning a joint diplomatic cold either: they'll conclude that things have become so awful that you need a week to a battle it out in. Before you know it you'll be forced into making a Public Appearance to put everyone's mind at rest, and then, of course, you're back at square one. Honestly, it's at times like this that you think Princess Di doesn't know what the cares of Public Life are all about, bless her. I mean, at least you don't get people dropping in to warm up the Fray Bentos pie they've just brought from the deli next door when you're getting intimate at Kensington Palace, do you?

Safety In Numbers

Although the ubiquity of other people can make brave girls wish they'd chosen their eight favourite discs and a luxury Jenkins and been packed off to late, great Roy Plomley's desert island years ago, it does have its plus side. It keeps the relationship fresh. After all, it's hard to get bored with someone if you hardly ever get the chance to talk to them, let alone enjoy hours of blissful conversation. On the other hand, if your social life is so hectic that the depth of your conversation doesn't extend beyond diary synchronising sessions, you may well wonder what you are doing attached to someone you barely know.

But even then all is not black; there's always that wonderful institution, the Country Weekend. All Jenkinses go off for country weekends with other Jenkinses from time to time and, as Official Consort, you will be included in the luggage. Actually the parties themselves can be an excrutiating trial if you aren't used to them, and anyway you're surrounded by people when you're there: no, the real glory of the event is the drive to and from the selected venue.

I know this statement may seem a little bizarre at first glance, but think about it. When you are thundering along the M11 at 80 mph nattering twenty-three to the dozen with the Delight of Your Life, there is little chance that you will be interrupted. Nobody can drop in for a quick drink and it is unlikely that the phone will ring unless your Jenkins is a gadget freak and has had one of those radio-powered numbers installed in the glove compartment of the old jalopy. Even if he has, you can always snap an essential wire or something (I know this is a slightly controversial piece of advice, but necessity is the mother of invention, or in this case destruction, and honestly, one *does* need to shut out the madding crowd every so often.)

At moments like these, the only thing likely to threaten your peace and quiet is the unwelcome intrusion of a fellow traveller. There's always somebody who wants a lift to the weekend retreat and unless you and Jenkins agree from the start that you won't take passengers, you may end up thinking that bus conductresses have more fun. The way to tackle the problem is to resort to foul play. This time Jenkins will probably be behind you all the way since he probably quite wants to be alone with you from time to time. He's only human after all.

The most effective method I have yet discovered is to embarrass the other passengers beyond belief. Sit behind Jenkins when he is driving, drape your arms gracefully around his neck and nibble his left ear. This lewd behaviour will make anyone else feel more than superfluous to say nothing of being frightened that Jenkins, unbalanced by your passion, will career into the hard shoulder. News of his unreliability will travel fast and soon all the faint-hearts will fall away. A word of caution though: don't nibble too hard or Jenkins may forget that you aren't doing this for fun and it could be dangerous.

Over the customary proceedings during these cosy drives I will draw a discreet veil. Suffice it to say that Jessica and a Jenkins once managed to make the journey from London to Norwich last for six hours and they weren't helped by traffic hold-ups, road-works or even big ends falling out. It struck her then that the whole ghastly Friday to Sunday fracas had been invented to give courting couples a chance. She may be wrong of course, but it's certainly not a rationalisation that can be easily disproved.

Sex Five: The Last Post

Assuming that you have passed the ordeal by friends, the question of marriage will probably be uppermost in your mind, and why not? When you've put so much effort into a relationship, the least you can expect is a few choice presents, a pretty frock and the heavenly choirboys humming 'Here comes the bride.'

Unfortunately, before you make it to the foot of the vicar, you will have to genuflect at Jenkins's family altar, because there's no chance of the chap making a union with you in the Eyes of God if in the eyes of the family you're the devil's only daughter.* It's a medieval approach I grant you, but then, what would you expect of one who has had the weight of duty placed so firmly on his shoulders – the ultimate responsibility being to continue the Line in the manner to which it has become accustomed.

In other words, if you think his friends were difficult enough to get to know you've got a terrible shock in store if you haven't yet met the family. In the steeple-chase of love, the biggest hurdle you'll have to jump for Jenkins is that of his nearest and dearest standing on each other's shoulders.

* There are one or two exceptions to prove this rule, but then all rules have exceptions and in this case I'm not going to go into them. If yours is the sort of Jenkins who is going to pooh-pooh the family, you're in luck, and the last thing you need is my advice!

Going to meet the family

The Deep End

Jenkinses have achieved world fame for many of their attributes, but one which has hitherto escaped attention is their subtlety. This could be because it isn't one of their strongest points, I suppose. When Jenkins suggests that you meet his family, it is tantamount to a proposal, even if he hasn't been through the old one-knee-exercise yet, and you'd better be aware of this. If you have any doubts about jogging towards eternity with Jenkins at your side, put off the whole event by any strategem you can devise. If feebler excuses fail, fall off your bicycle and break a few limbs; the transitory pain this will engender will be as nought to the recurring nightmare the alternative can bring. If this sounds a little like a hysterical reaction to you, go ahead, try it. Then we'll see which side of your face you're laughing on, my girl.

And remember, once the news gets out that you have been served up to the Jenkins family with their Sunday luncheon, there may be no going back. Friends will hear the sound of distant wedding bells and start to stockpile rice. They will not be pleased if they find they have turned their larders into neatly packed paddy fields for nothing. Going to meet the family is going in at the deep end, make no mistake about it. Don't just hold your nose and jump blindly – you're bound to do a belly flop.

Testing The Water

Even if Jenkins's family aren't famous for their impersonations of predators they can easily forget their manners and perform a passable imitation of a pride of hungry lions. With a bit of luck Jenkins will know this and he won't throw you into the centre of the den straight away. Instead he'll attempt to get you acquainted with the species by wheeling out a few of the tamer beasts: his brothers. These are not to be trifled with, but to be charmed; they may be useful later. Unfortunately, however, their opinions about you are not to be relied upon, for they will carry no weight with their women-folk. This may surprise you, but that's the way it is. You'll just have to learn to adapt, for if you are what the prison fraternity refer to as a lifer, sooner or later you will have to get to grips with the fact that though Jenkins may be planning to marry you and you alone, you are scheduled to marry him and his family. You poor mutt.

The heavy jelly course will be introduced casually at first. 'My sister is coming to town next week. It's a terrible bore but she wants me to have dinner with her. You wouldn't care to come with me, would you?' This is a fairly standard way for him to introduce the torture, because he knows that if he seems to be asking a favour, your mouth will say yes before your brain has even clocked on for the evening. Fools rush in where angels wouldn't be seen dead.

Before you cry tush, avast, tommy rot, I would like to remind you that I know what I'm talking about. Not only have I been in your position myself, I can also speak from the vantage point of being a Jenkins sister. And it may interest you to know that though I have suffered the slings and arrows of other peoples's sisters' tongues, as far as my own brother is concerned, I have mellowed not a jot.

As far as I and all my kind are concerned, our own Jenkinses are the finest creatures ever to have lolled across God's earth. OK, OK, I may occasionally lend him out, and from time to time appear to have no kind word to waste upon the ghastly little oik, but let me tell you that should you insinuate that you also think he is an international disaster zone, I will adopt a truly Jenkins-like stand and thump you. Only sisters are allowed to despise Jenkinses, and anyone else showing similar distaste is apt to have her nose rearranged.

No, as far as I can see, Aphrodite herself would be hard-pushed to convince me she was good enough for my brother. On the other hand, if you're out there, Aphro baby, I'll try to give you a fair hearing. I wouldn't like to condemn the poor boy to terminal bachelordom.

Furthermore, having met myself in the form of other Jenkins's sisters, I can assure you that this sort of attitude makes it tough going for prospective sisters-in-law. If you are somewhat defective in the grey matter, you will be met with 'Oh, you're a secretary are you, dear? Tell me, what make *is* your lipstick. It's such a pretty colour.' Or if you are bright: 'Jenkins tells me you went to university. You're not interested in having children, then?' Whichever category you fall into, you won't exactly be given a lot of scope to prove what a truly wonderful person you are.

However, as with all other things in Jenkinsdom, so with his sister: perseverance will win the day. If you manage to stick around for a twelvemonth or so, the dear girls will accept you out of sheer admiration for your leather-like skin. You will know you are part of the family when they start to involve you in subtle plots to help Jenkins to discover the true meaning of a toothbrush's life. After that, it's all for one and one for all in the fight against halitosis, and you can start to practise signing cheques with a new surname.

The Thinnest Ice Of All

Difficult though the qualifying round may be, the finale is the pits. Please, please, under no circumstances get yourself shanghai-ed into being left alone with Mummy. The horrors of the experience are so variously dreadful that I get a fit of the stammers just thinking about them. For whatever Mummy is looking for, chances are you aren't it. Worse still, Jenkins is inclined to trust her judgement implicitly. You must realise that in his eyes, his mother is more or less the Holy Virgin and Athene rolled into one. This is largely due to the fact that he doesn't know her very well, having been away at school for most of his life, cherishing a vision of the ideal Mamma. Of course, some would say that a woman who sends her son away to school before he can lisp is hardly the personification of the maternal spirit, but for goodness sake, don't mention this to Jenkins. He'll only think you're an anti-Christ or something.

Anyway, all his mother wants from you is an absolute adoration of her son combined with a working knowledge of all his faults, the cure for these, and a crusading zeal about his career. You should also be totally devoted to him, an independent girl, ready to administer to his every whim while holding down a steady job, at least until you begin to whelp. If you *can* contrive to do all these things at once you are suffering from a chronic identity crisis and the last thing you should be looking for is a husband: a good shrink would be much more useful.

Even if you can manage to fulfill all the above requirements, it will do you no good. The whole sad issue puts me in mind of my lacrimose friend Rowena. She was never a head-strong girl, Rowena, in fact there have been times when she's been so insipid that I have been tempted to colour her in. Nevertheless there's not an ounce of harm in her, and when she fell in love it was with the self-effacing thud we all expected. Supernovas sped across her eyes and you could almost see hearts and flowers spilling out of her ears like they do on those nauseating cards they print for Valentine's Day. It all went well until she was invited to sit at Jenkins's country seat for a weekend. Oh! the pity of it. The returnee was not so much a girl as a shred. After three days' silence during which many of her friends wondered if she had stepped on a UXB down there in Wiltshire and had resultant shell-shock, she moved her parched lips to ask for water. Recognising this to be a conversational gambit, I piled in and asked her why she hadn't called in the bomb disposal experts instead of tackling the job herself.

She blinked a bit, her eyes a-brim with tears and then, somewhat incongruously, I felt, said 'Oh, Beccs! I wouldn't wish Mrs Jenkins on anyone, let alone the paras.'

I gave her a cigarette, to remind her she was in an English speaking country, and that helped her coherence.

'I did everything she wanted, the old *ding* bat! Everything. Even said that I voted Tory, wanted masses of children and supported the "Campaign for People against the Population Explosion". I told her I hunted foxes but really felt blood sports were wrong. I said whatever she seemed to want me to, and do you know what? *Do* you know what? She told Jenkins he'd be mad to marry a fuzzy little no-brained half-wit who contradicted herself the whole time and didn't know her own mind. And *he* said he saw her point.'

So did I, but this was not the time to tell Rowena. However, I will tell *you* that a conversation with Jenkins's mother is peppered with fiancée-traps. Furthermore, the dear dowagers plan them for years. I related the above woeful history to my own mother, and to my horror she clicked her tongue and said she thoroughly approved of the ogress of the piece. Somewhat unsettled I asked her how she'd handle my own brother's prospective wife, should there ever be one. She folded her arms; a self-sastisfied smile travelled from jowl to jowl; and she told me. I won't go into detail, but I can tell you, she's going to be horrid as hell!

Mind you, there are rare instances where all goes well, and for once I was one of the lucky ones. Not that I deserved to be, mind you, since I'd been staying with Jenkins while his parents were away. At last the awful evening came when they returned and I had to meet them. I was so nervous that, though I've never been tall for my age, I felt I had shrunk to half my former height. Jenkins gave me a final wink and what was probably an encouraging smile, but it's always hard to tell what's going on 1½ feet above your head so I mistook it for a grimace. Thus encouraged we sallied forth.

'Well, Tristram, where's this girl we've heard so much about?' said a gentle voice as Jenkins's six foot six frame blocked the doorway.

He coughed with embarrassment, which didn't make me feel much better, then stood aside. There was a silence followed by a vast peal of laughter. I shrank another foot.

'Well, nature's obviously decided to even out the balance as far as height's concerned, thank goodness,' said Mrs Jenkins when she'd stopped and dried her mirthful tears.

'And I'm so pleased dear, that Tris isn't keeping that tiny evening dress in his wardrobe for himself.' Whereat she kissed me, God rest her generous soul.

If your Jenkins's Mum is of this sort, hang on in there. Nothing bad can come of it!

Cresting The Wave

If there is one thing to keep you going through the whole family ordeal, it's Jenkins's Papa. Mr Jenkins will be pre-disposed to like you, and since his son will be an updated carbon copy of the original, you shouldn't find him hard to like in return. Charm him a bit, laugh at his prehistoric jokes and you'll have a friend for life. He will also be a staunch ally, for he will know of old just how difficult the rest of his family can be. So when the going gets rough, he'll offer you a welcome refuge. Course, you may have to learn how to pull clay pigeons before he really warms to you, but when you consider the advantages, this is a very small price to pay.

The Logical Conclusion

If you can pass the family test you may well find Jenkins offering all his worldly goods till death doth you part. Well done!

If you accept, I wish you the best of British luck! Not that you'll need it, of course. Oh, and when you're kneeling down, giving the 'I do' your all, remember it's all so that one day you can have a little Jenkins just like his daddy, your spouse. Do treat the little fellow kindly, there's a good girl. After all, he's got a difficult act to follow.

Apologia

There are those who, having read this book, may wonder why I said the English Public Schoolboy was something special and worth preserving. After all, I have hardly painted him with a rose-tinted brush. In fact from all I have said, you might be left with the impression that he is an unwashed, uncivilised, unlovable hoodlum without a grace to save him. If this is the case, I am awfully sorry. You have been grossly misled, and I have also failed to convey the fact that I am the first registered Jenkins-junkie on the list.

In mitigation I would contend that I did not set out to write an advertising compaign. Had I done so I daresay you would be already out rooting through your local Bargain Basement in search of a slightly soiled Jenkins Min. But I did say that I was only trying to help the besotted female understand why the man is only 90% Prince Charming and 10% Premier Qualitie Great Oaf. After all, it's only when the Great Oaf bits are prominent that you need a guiding word. If the Course of True Love were running smooth, the last thing you'd be doing is hanging round the place reading books.

Whatever I say, however, there are bound to be a few doubting Thomasinas out there who will want to know why they should bother in the first place. Difficult question. The only answer I can think of is that Jenkins is a glorious, intriguing, complicated challenge. You accept the challenge because you have an adventurous spirit and because, as Sir Edmund Hilary said, it's there. Or maybe you just have a natural urge to dominate the indomitable.

Anyway, you will be well rewarded. Once conquered, Jenkins is the most perfect of perfect gentlemen. He is kind, and, when he remembers, considerate. Mind you he can take it to extremes and leave you wondering if the wicked fairy visited you and made you breakable overnight, so delicately will you be treated. Furthermore, Jenkins will never let you down. You could be on the other side of the world in a dreadfully silly scrape and after a quick phone call to Jenkins you will find that somehow he'll have you on your way home in no time. Or, if he isn't thinking straight that morning, he'll get the next plane out to share the mess with you, even though you might have chucked him three years ago. For Jenkins, dear soul, firmly imagines that it is his duty in life to charge about helping damsels in distress. On the other hand, if you don't state the problem simply and clearly he may well fail to notice that there's anything on your frail female mind at all, and that you've reversed the charges from downtown Jakarta for a social call.

Having read that, you will probably assume that Jenkins holds despicably unliberated views about women, and again, you'd be wrong. If you want to fight for your equality, he'll be there in the firing line with you, not least because of the fear that his absence may cause you to make an unpleasant scene in public. He will even read the odd feminist tract if he thinks it'll save him embarrassment. Also, if you have a talent or ambition he won't come out in male chauvinist spots. He might feel bewildered at first, but he will soon remember that women are well known for being confusing and then give you full support. If you succeed in your ventures he will be as pleased as Punch and tell everyone how wonderful you are. Course, he may imply that he put the idea into your pretty head to start with, but this is only because he doesn't want anyone to think you're unfemininely pushy or a freak. I did mention, I think, that he can be loyal to this sort of fault.

At best he is witty, amusing and unswervingly honest. At worst he is just plain odd. His major failing is to bring out the gentlewoman in you which could have you rushing to rescue your bra from the flames just when he was learning that women are tougher than they used to be. If you get burned, it's your own fault. Me and your mother both have warned you not to play with fire.

Final Warning

If there is any chance your knees would buckle if someone nuzzled the nape of your neck, be very careful. If there is even the slightest suspicion that, should those nuzzles travel down your spine, you would buckle to the logical conclusion, be very very careful. And if you but hypothesise that you would be undeterred, be you in a car park off the Finchley Road, or on top of a Cliff of Mohir, be warned: you are very unlikely to find total and lasting fulfilment with Jenkins.

Why? Jenkins and his papa were brought up to believe that you can more or less do what you want, as long as it doesn't frighten the horses, as I think I told you. What I may not have added is that the horses in Jenkinshire are amongst the most timorous quadrupeds in the history of mammals. And it's no good telling me that you seldom run into a herd of wild Neddies in South Hampstead: I know that, but logic never works with you know who. The grim truth remains that you have just admitted to yearnings that would give the steed of your present paramour a coronary. Canter off, while the going's good.

You may wonder that I can speak with such authority. But then you don't know what happened to Jessica. So I will tell you. Jessica, as you may recall, was a girl with a dangerous amount of lip until she discovered her neck. Well, actually, someone else discovered it for her and his name was nothing like Tristram.

The effect has been staggering. Gone are the navy blue tights, matching skirt, knickers, bra and Renault. And in their place, a whole woman.

And don't get me wrong: we're not talking simple sex here. We are talking the wild unleashings of creative and philosophical passion, as well as the old horizontal Charleston. Yes, really, you can take it from me, I've known Jessica woman and brat for longer than I care to remember. And we've a lot more in common than meets the eye.

In other words, Jess hasn't pulled clay for a Jenkins in oh, four years. She looks back on her time in the land of lobbed peas as a kind of acid trip without the pretty colours.

I only tell you this because its true.

Very last word

Things have changed since I first wrote this book. Quite the most surprising is that I contrived to grow up. Yes, I know, shocking. And in the process, I grew out of the tribe of Jenkins. Well, I still love m'brother (but then, who wouldn't? Have you *seen* the child since it turned into a man? No? Just as well. There's enough swooning done in Hollywood without you starting.)

But don't let me put you off. If you are going to

match and hatch before you despatch, fair play to you: I'm all for preserving endangered species. And I'll always have a soft spot for Jenkins, his dog, and my old one-eared teddy. But when it comes to the finer arts of living, I tell you what, a Buddhist is far more fun.

Also available from Mandarin Paperbacks

JILLY COOPER

How To Stay Married

Jilly Cooper's good-humoured and witty guide to surviving the married state was originally written and boldly published when the author herself was only recently married. It contains a wealth of shrewd advice on such matters as 'Setting Up House', 'Relations and Friends', 'Sex', 'Clothes' and 'Affairs'. Two decades later this pithy account of what makes married people tick can claim to have acquired classic status, and amongst the many surviving marriages which have benefitted from the author's wisdom may be counted the author's own.

ERMA BOMBECK

I Lost Everything In The Post-Natal Depression

'Before you read this book, there are a few things you should know about me. I consider ironed sheets a health hazard.
Children should be judged on what they are – a punishment for an early marriage.
For years, I have worked at being a simple, average housewife. I am ready to face the facts. I'm a loser.'

Celebrated columnist and bestselling author of *The Grass is Always Greener over the Septic Tank* and *If Life is a Bowl of Cherries – What Am I Doing in the Pits?*, Erma Bombeck is distinctly dubious about the joys of motherhood and family life.

Acerbic, witty and delightfully jaundiced, she has an unerring eye for the humour of domestic traumas.

'A sharp and very funny lady . . . right on target'
Publishers Weekly

'A phenomenon . . . who manages to hit everybody's funny bone'
Newsweek

'There is truth in the best of her humour, as well as sanity'
New York Times